Black Dog Publishing
London New York

THE COFFEE TABLE COFFEE TABLE BOOK

Alexander Payne // James Zemaitis

When you Google the expression "coffee table" on the Internet, over 2,160,000 entries are listed. So what is a coffee table? Where to start? When we first began discussing a book on coffee tables for a coffee table, it was clear that there was a need for a celebratory compendium on the greatest examples of the coffee table in twentieth century design.

The coffee table has become a fixture of the home in the twentieth century. What shag-carpeted post collegiate crash pad doesn't have one, covered with beer cans, TV remotes, overflowing ashtrays and fast-food containers, surrounded by sagging stained sofas? What Bright Young Thing on the Upper East Side or in Notting Hill doesn't rely on one to display the books on Helmut Newton and Mapplethorpe, the Orrefors bowl filled with coloured stones, the pruned bonsai tree? What urban environment photographed in the ubiquitous interior magazines for the *Wallpaper* generation doesn't have at least two or three of them?

Jean Royère
project for the Salon à la maison
de France à Rio de Janeiro, circa 1950
pencil and gouache on Canson paper

We thought we would give our readers a few definitions:

Coffee table · n. a small, low table.

Coffee table book · n. a large lavishly illustrated book, especially one intended only for casual reading.

Coffee table · not a contemporary term, and not a specialised article. Generally applicable to any small, light occasional table. What is often known today as a coffee table was originally a tea kettle stand.

Coffee table book · a supplementary function of the coffee table in the United States is for the casual display of two or three selected books, to suggest cultural status. The term "coffee table book" is American and became current in the 1950s; but this form of showing-off is common to all countries in circles where spurious values encourage a reverence for status symbols.

2. JAM
Flatscreen Coffee Tables, 1999
Using a widescreen from a
Sony Wega television, JAM
asked fellow artists and
designers to create artworks
under the screen.

With these definitions in mind, and
with an academic eye, we've selected
over 130 icons of the coffee table. Of
course, there are the mass-produced
stone-cold classics, such as Isamu
Noguchi's IN-50—perhaps *the* coffee
table, and more an expression of
freeform sculpture, an abstract
aesthetic masterpiece from the mid-
century, than merely somewhere to
place your coffee cup. As well, there
are the rarities that any collector
would hack off a limb or sell mother
to possess—Noguchi's prototype for
the IN-50, the A Conger Goodyear
table, to which our cover design pays
tribute. Most of the selected works
fall somewhere in between, from
superb stalwarts that epitomise an
age, (again, Noguchi's IN-52 'rudder'
table comes to mind, but we promise,
there are other designers here as
well) to minor masterpieces by
designers who haven't yet been
rediscovered by collectors.

A Herman Miller advertising shot
for moulded plywood furniture
by Charles and Ray Eames, circa 1948.

Our finished product, *The Coffee Table Coffee Table Book*, is a humble attempt at an
academic guide that will also hopefully impress house guests when placed on the
reader's own coffee table. For the generation who watched *Seinfeld* in the 1990s, this
might stir memories of the legendary episode when Kramer designed a coffee table book
that becomes its own coffee table, which he demonstrated to ensuing mayhem on the
morning talk show *Live with Regis and Kathy Lee*. In fact, the Boym Studio in New York
deserves credit for being the first to design such a monster in 1992, when they married
coffee table books with plywood legs taken from furniture available in the Sears
catalogue. At any rate, when we looked at our design libraries and saw nothing but
endless books fetishising the chair, we sprung into action.

When is a coffee table a coffee table? It seems to be defined by its role in the room—an
ordinary low table becoming one when taken into a living/drawing room, lounge or salon
and used as an object on which to place coffee table books and cups of coffee. It is made
distinct by its form, height, and use. And when does a wine rack, palette or door become
a coffee table? Why, when it is placed in front of a sofa, or the classic three-piece suite.
That is, as long as it is constructed at the desired height and used for the requisite
purpose, sometimes providing a feeding trough between couch potatoes and the TV, other
times as the genuine centre of social intercourse, to centre the spatial arrangement
around which a few hipsters can drink and smoke. Since the 1920s, the one thing that all
coffee tables have in common is their height—approximately 16 - 24 inches high. Styles
have ranged from bizarre miniaturised 'Regency' or 'Georgian' examples to the avant-
garde. If one were to pick the two most enduring forms of the coffee table, one would
probably pick a rectangle and an amoeba. But the coffee table can take virtually any
form, and stretch the limits of both the imagination and good taste, from rustic barn
door to media centre, from sci-fi fantasy to an actual work of art.

Jacques-Emile Ruhlmann
Boudoir-library, 1918

16

During the nineteenth century the occasional table was placed behind the seating furniture; the group of seats was arranged around the fireplace, the main focus of the room being the supplier of heat and light. The fireplace would have been adorned with a mantelpiece sporting a clock, and above that a large over mantle mirror, which would reflect candlelight. Somehow, the occasional table turned into the coffee table, the Modern object of the twentieth century, the centrepiece of the living room, taking pride of place in front of the sofa. It has become the command centre for the modern age, a platform from which to launch the vices of the late twentieth century—tv, hi-fi and video via remote controls.

The coffee table now serves as an impromptu dining table, on which we wolf down our microwaved meals and enjoy a flick on the Spice Channel. And now, in the twenty-first century, it has become an altar, where one displays one's social and cultural aspirations by the careful placement of cautiously chosen stacks of coffee table books (in an aesthetically pleasing order), groupings of works of art, with little space for the coffee. Indeed, in films, advertising and the plethora of home style and decoration books, we can look to the objects on the coffee table to understand something of the person living in a particular the environment and their aspiration to a certain social standing.

Coffee and its accessories have come a long way. Coffee originated in Turkey in the sixteenth century and was transported to the coffee houses of London in the seventeenth century when, coffee drinking became fashionable. The first coffee house in London was opened circa 1652, where the patrons rested their manuscripts of the day on oak joint stools. The eighteenth and nineteenth centuries saw the table evolve from a tripod table for coffee and other drinks to the occasional table as tastes and styles of entertaining changed. In the twentieth century, the coffee table originated as an elite object of the French salons of the 1920s and 30s, as part of interiors containing the drama and grandeur of designs by Emile-Jacques Ruhlmann, Jean-Michel Frank or Armand-Albert Rateau. However, from the start, the coffee table was never destined to become exclusively a solitary elitist object, since concurrently to the French salons, Depression-era Americans could purchase low-cost examples from Sears-Roebuck. Today, this contrast between high and low continues, as one can buy a coffee table from Ikea for a hundred pounds, or spend upwards of a hundred thousand at auction on one by the French masters. From Swedish low-cost design to Hollywood glamour, there's a coffee table for every environment.

IKEA of Sweden—design team
Lack, circa 2001
The ubiquitous Ikea look has
become the quick fix for fresh
modern design, producing items
synonymous for everyone,
ranging from the college low
budget solution to the first time
buyer in dire need of furniture.
The design has an anonymous
look to it—conservative modern
for the masses.

David Barquist notes that, "During the late nineteenth and early twentieth centuries, the term coffee table was used to describe small, low tables on which coffee services could be placed. These tables were frequently designed in vaguely Near Eastern or North African styles as components of 'Turkish' interiors, since coffee drinking was associated with those regions, such rooms often functioned as a place to serve coffee after a meal." Barquist adds that the coffee table "was essentially an updated version of the nineteenth century centre table; several sources recommend cutting down old centre tables for use as coffee tables".

So when, in fact, did the first true coffee table, as we know it, appear, and when was the term first used? Certainly the popularity of the term seems to have come from America and the 1950s (as one of our 'definitions', above, attests to), but its inspirations and origins come

from Europe. European furniture designs of the 1920s, which we would today catalogue as coffee tables, were originally marketed under such terms as "low", or "occasional" tables. And for all of the research that we could provide on the various Turkish-inspired coffee tables of the preceding centuries, the fact remains that, in the 1920s, Europeans first started designing the direct ancestors of today's coffee tables without really knowing what to call them. It was the Americans and the English who defined and transformed the coffee table in the 1930s and 1940s into the form that we know today.

In America in the 1950s the coffee table merged into the 'living landscape' as an expression of "Good Design" for the Post War generation of middle class consumers who, for the first time, owned their own homes. During the late 1950s and 60s we saw the advent of the coffee bar, made famous by the Italian culture brought

to us by films such as Roman Holiday and still evident today in the mecca for coffee-consuming, Bar Italia in Soho, London. More recently, perhaps because the coffee table in the home has become revered as an object devoted to and a part of high style and taste—coffee drinking has left the home and taken up residence in the high street and shopping centre. This, of course, is also due to the fact that life, generally, has become more rushed and fast-paced; it is more convenient to meet friends or colleagues for a coffee whilst on the move than to return home. Convenience is at the centre here—it is easier to "pop out" to buy a coffee than to make one. And so we've come full-circle, as the coffee that comes near its namesake table in our home might quite likely be in a paper cup, emblazoned with a Starbucks logo.

4. Isamu Noguchi
IN-52, 1949

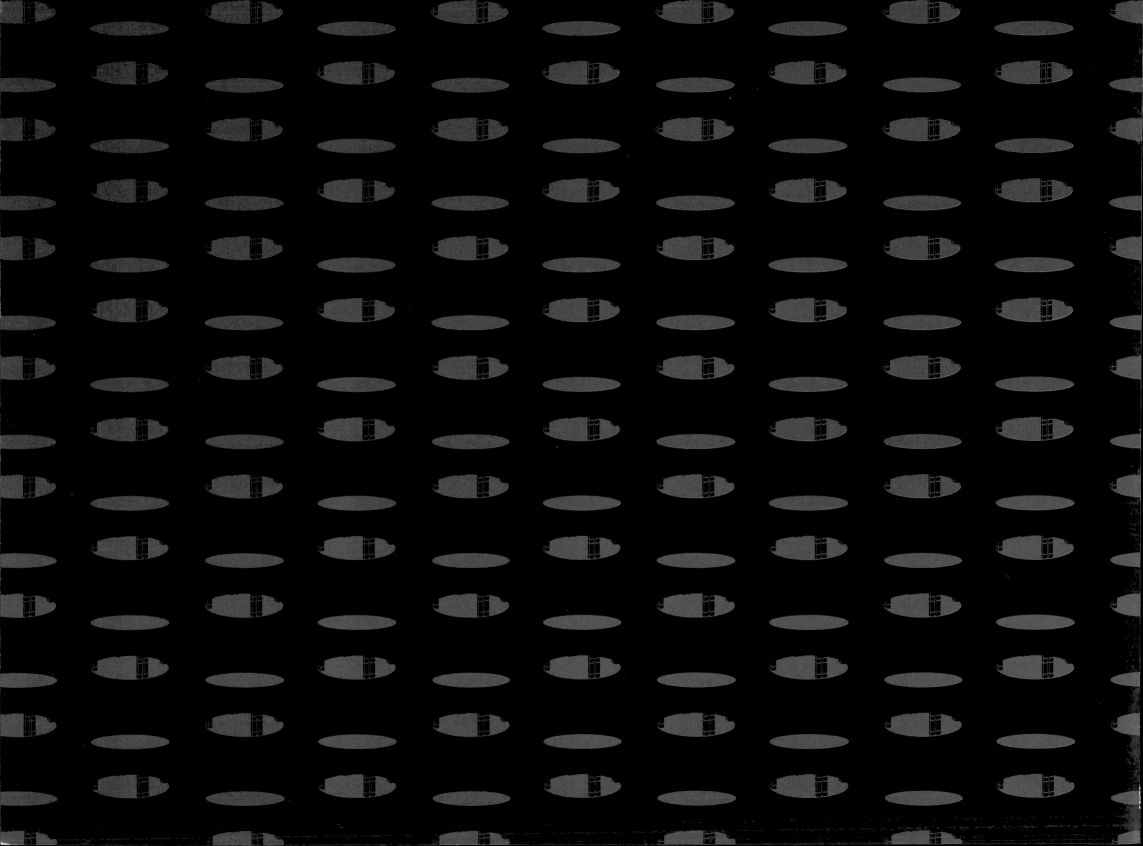

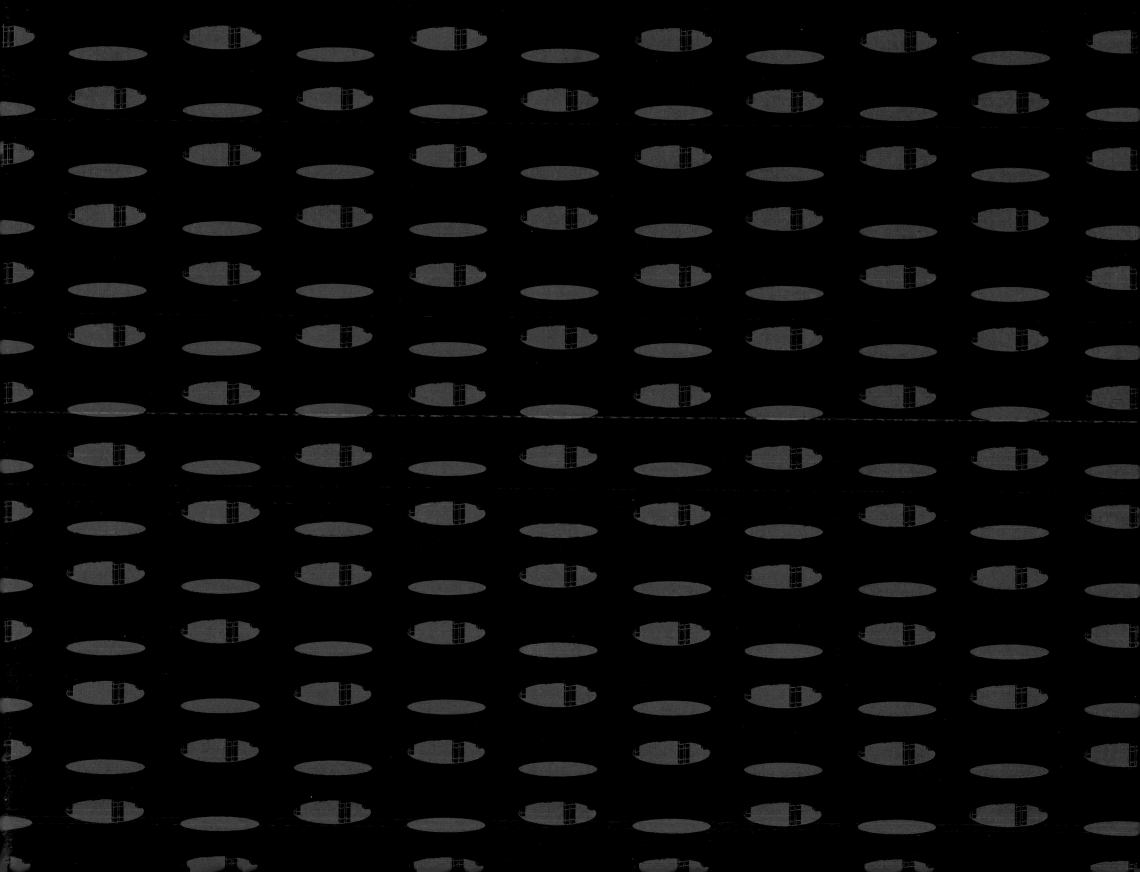

two

Starting in 1915, the young Eileen Gray, who had made her Parisian Salon debut in 1913, designed a table with African-inspired legs and a red and silver-lacquered bilboquet (cup and ball) decoration on its top for her first important client, the extraordinarily wealthy couturier Jacques Doucet. This table, arguably, might be seen as the protoype for all modernist circular tables, although Gray placed it off to one side of a Marcel Coard sofa, typifying the French aversion to placing anything on top of the central rug.

In 1918, Emile-Jacques Ruhlmann placed a basse bouille—a long low table—at the centre of a seating group in the Paris apartment of Fernande Cabanel. Armand Rateau placed perhaps the most famed low table of the era in front of the fireplace in the living room of Jeanne Lanvin, designed 1920-1922. This bronze masterpiece derived from the antique represents the apex of Art Deco wealth and exuberance. But in general the French masters were far more preoccupied with dressing up the traditional forms of dining tables,

consoles, nesting tables and occasional tables to really put much emphasis into redesigning their salon lifestyle to incorporate a form that we now consider an essential design element of Modernity.

5. Eileen Gray
Bilboquet table, circa 1915
This important early design
represented a bold new step in
the interior. It preceded the
basse bouille of Ruhlmann by
three years.

Jacques Doucet's salon
late 1920s
Published in L'Illustration,
May 1930, showing the Bilboquet
table in situ. It was designed
for the salon in his Neuily
studio. Doucet was Gray's first
major patron.

6. Jacques-Emile Ruhlmann
basse bouille, 1918-1919

Jacques-Emile Ruhlmann
Apartment for the dress
designer Fernarde Cabanel, the
photograph shows the basse
bouille table.

Jacques-Emile Ruhlmann
chambre de jeune fils featuring the
Colonette table basse, circa 1920-22

7. Jacques-Emile Ruhlmann
Colonette table basse, circa 1920-22
A low table with under-tier in
macassar ebony. Ruhlmann
produced other versions of this
model in burl amboyna, ash and
oak.

Charlotte Perriand
le Bars sous le Toit, 1927
Shown at the Salon d'Autome,
Paris.

Yet it was the chic juxtaposition of historicism and modernism that provided American visitors to the seminal 1925 Paris Exposition des Art Decoratifs et Industriels Modernes with a Gallic kick in the pants. Up to this point, American furniture companies had begun to understand the need for a new form and a new social setting, but opted instead to dismember nineteenth century table styles by amputating their legs. Thus, in 1922, the Grand Rapids Furniture Company (a holdover from the Arts and Crafts movement that later went 'moderne' with Kem Weber) produced a Rococo Revival style table that historians inform us is one of the first American coffee table designs. However, following the 1925 Exposition, American manufacturers hadn't quite figured things out yet, so they attempted blatant homages to the cliché of French Art Deco style, as seen in furniture designed by The Company of Master Craftsman, a New York firm that exhibited at the Waldorf-Astoria in 1926.

Francis Jourdain
Project de Studio, circa 1925-1930
gouache on paper

Meanwhile, French decorators of the 1920s continued to periodically incorporate coffee tables into their interiors, although always describing them as "table basse". Exotic woods and superb craftsmanship were always essential. Jean-Michel Frank led the way with rectangular tables covered in galuchat, mica, parchment and straw parquetries. In the early 1920s, Ruhlmann had designed the circular Colonists table in sumptuous ebene de macassar and ivory, which he would continue to use in numerous commissions and exhibition rooms throughout the decade. And in the widely circulated modernist architectural drawings in gouache by

Francois Jourdain, there appear on several occasions centralised tables adorned with coffee services, although these tables are usually a bit higher than what one would expect. French modernist architects, however, weren't necessarily on the same page. For example, there really isn't a good example of a coffee table by Pierre Chareau or Robert Mallet-Stevens. The Pavillon de l'Espirit Nouveau designed by Le Corbusier and Pierre Jeanneret for the 1925 Exposition is devoid of any forms even remotely resembling coffee tables. There was no place for a coffee table in "The Machine for Living".

But in 1927, there appears a stunningly geometric, machine-age design that anticipated the first onslaught of coffee table designs by Donald Deskey and other American modernists of the late 1920s and early 30s—Charlotte Perriand's table in her interior Le Bar sous le Toit. It is also the use for Perriand's table—cocktails, not coffee—that would prove to be a major inspiration for American tables of the next decade.

8. Jean-Michel Frank
table basse, circa 1930
The earliest and most iconic of
Frank's low table designs,
produced in shagreen (shown
here) as well as parchment.

The theories and designs of the Bauhaus were not on view in Paris, as there remained a strong anti-German sentiment dating back to World War One. But in Germany the word Kaffeetisch appears in an article in Für Haus. The Bauhaus masters never used the term, opting for such descriptions as Blumentisch (flower table) and Teetisch (tea table). But the designs of Ludwig Mies van der Rohe and Marcel Breuer from the late 1920s inspired generations of reproductions and bastardisations by the English and American furniture industry. From the tubular-steel craze of the 1930s, which spawned low table designs in the hundreds, pumped out by Thonet in Europe, PEL (Practical Equipment Limited) in England, and various American firms including Lloyd and Royale, to the Knoll reissues of the Post War era, it is simply amazing how far-reaching these few designs by Mies van der Rohe and Breuer would prove to be.

In particular, it is especially astonishing how Mies' table for the Barcelona Pavilion, designed in 1928 (and reissued and renamed by Knoll), has become perhaps the most popular coffee table of Post War 'modernist' interiors, especially in its preferred role as the quintessential table of waiting areas—from apartment lobbies to doctors' offices—where it is usually accompanied by tandems of Barcelona chairs.

10. Ludwig Mies van der Rohe
Barcelona table, originally
designed 1929
the Knoll International reissue,
from 1948 onwards is pictured here.

11. Ludwig Mies van der Rohe
Tugendhat table
originally designed 1930
the Knoll International reissue,
from 1964 onwards is pictured here.

12. Ludwig Mies van der Rohe
table for the Barcelona Pavilion, Berlin 1928
Believed to be the only surviving work from
the Pavilion, this historic design was recently
acquired by the Neue Galerie,
New York

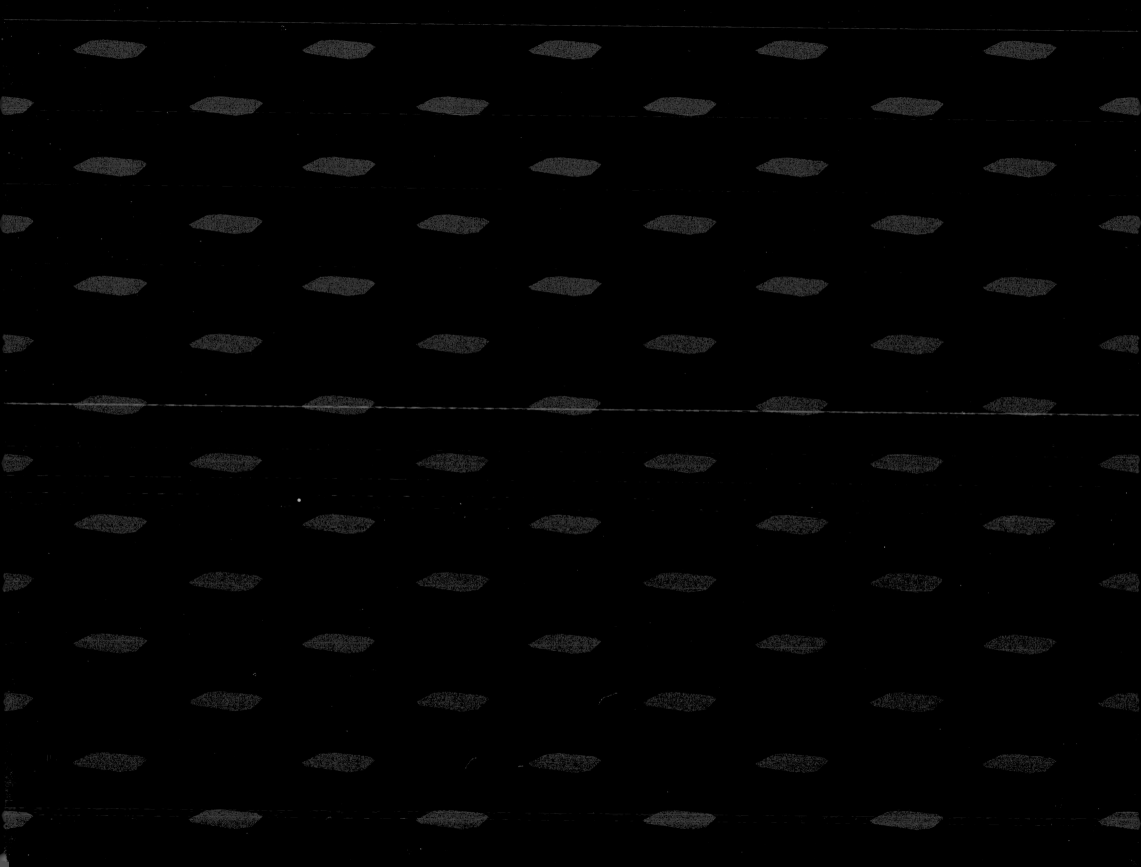

three

from cocktails to the Goodyears

In the 1930s, although somewhat responsible in the previous decade for the first coffee table designs, French architects and decorators were oblivious when it came to developing new styles of the table basse. Whether it was a modernist rectangular gem by Marc du Plantier or Paul Dupre-Lafon, a pastiche of neoclassicism by the decorating firms Jansen or Ramsay, or an ornamental crime by Gilbert Poillerat, the French would stick with traditional salon-style living arrangements until the end of the Second World War.Consequently, their coffee table designs were infrequent and rarely avant-garde in form.

But America, where the lessons of the 1925 Exposition were supplemented by a tidal wave of Austrian and German designers flooding New York and Los Angeles, was fertile ground for the development of the coffee table. In 1930, a group of young designers, mostly based in New York, formed the American Union of Decorative Artists and Craftsmen (AUDAC) as a means of promoting their furniture, textiles and industrial designs. Their aim was to bring the Bauhaus to your house, yet not without a nod to Francophile tastes. American-born members included Donald Deskey, Gilbert Rohde, Frank Lloyd Wright and Russel Wright, while amongst the immigrants were Paul Frankl, Frederick Kiesler and Kem Weber. Their first exhibition was held in the same year, and while few designs that could be considered coffee tables were included in the room settings, a mood of modernity and urbanity, coupled with a new appreciation of industry and the machine, marked the birth of American Modernism. The coffee table would, nevertheless, play a considerable role in the efficacy of this movement.

13. Donald Deskey
cocktail table, 1927-1931
A 1930 *Home and Field* article noted that "It was
Prohibition which invented a new use for a new
piece of furniture—the cocktail table—something
with a low center of gravity, not top-heavy, and
easily cleaned." Deskey later replaced the
Vitrolite glass tops to this design with Bakelite,
commenting in 1934, "I used plastics for the first
time as a table top in a room I designed for a
private client, and chose that material because
of its resistance to cigarette burns and because it
was the only suitable material that could
withstand the alcoholic concoctions of that era."

Much of this newly innovative American Modernism was based on streamlining and
skyscraper motifs. Nonetheless, these twin pillars of American industrial might—speed
and verticality—were difficult to translate into coffee tables. Paul Frankl, who was the
inaugural and most aggressive purveyor of skyscraper modernism, designed numerous
bookcases and desks that, "moving upward" through stepped-up, setback progressions,
were imitative of the towering structures of Manhattan. But in the late 1920s, in his
classic treatise New Dimensions, Frankl reverted to Chinese revivalism when it came to
designing a "low, mirror-topped table" for a showroom at Abraham & Straus. And
streamlining worked best in household objects, from soda siphons to meat slicers. By
contrast, coffee tables seemed hopelessly conservative, their role limiting any radical
design changes.

Paul Frankl
a modern living Room from an exhibition at Abraham & Straus,
Brooklyn, illustrated in Paul Frankl, *New Dimensions*, 1928
In another 1928 article, Frankl wrote "low tables connote
informality, recumbent or semi-recumbent intimacy—in a
word, complete relaxation."

14. Gilbert Rhode
Rotorette, 1929
The Rotorette was exhibited in
the 1930 AUDAC exhibition. The
cellarette's four sections were
officially meant for books,
glassware and bottles. But who
hides their books?

44

Of course, the 1930s also began with America mired in the Great Depression and restrictions of Prohibition. Drinking was driven underground to speakeasies or kept behind closed doors in private parties held at home. But ironically, the latter enabled Americans to expand their cultural palette and encouraged new forms of socialisation, from a flexibility and informality in seating arrangements to outrageous and colourful cocktails (often to disguise the use of toxic bathtub gin). At the same time, there was a clandestine element to home entertainment. Cocktail shakers were sometimes disguised as coffee pots. And while some low tables were overtly marketed to the bibulous crowd by Donald Deskey's firm as "cocktail tables", others, such as Gilbert Rohde's Rotorette table, 1929, were designed with secret compartments for hiding the hooch.

Russel Wright's living room,
East 40th Street, New York, circa 1937
The revolving coffee table pictured
here was retained by Wright in all of
his various apartments in New York.
Considering how frequently his own
rooms appeared in the 'shelter'
magazines of the day, the collector
William Straus has maintained that
this is the most photographed table of
the era.

Walter Dorwin Teague
sitting room for La Société Matford,
Paris, 1930s
A conservative Francophile approach
to the form by one of America's
most prominent industrial designers
and champion of streamlining.

When Prohibition was repealed in December 1933 (President Roosevelt downed a martini in
public to celebrate) it was as if a license was suddenly granted for Americans to entertain
publicly, casually, and exuberantly. The floodgates opened, and there was an outpouring
of low tables, mostly in tubular steel, ranging from elitist designs for socialites'
apartments to low-cost examples manufactured by large Midwestern firms. A prominent
furniture designer of the period was Warren McArthur, who opened a showroom at One Park
Avenue in New York after a period spent in Los Angeles designing outdoor furniture for
Hollywood starlets. McArthur's signature designs in tubular aluminium, derived from
Breuer but fraught with a kinetic, uniquely American industrial mark, were tailored to
upscale apartment dwellers. His catalogue offered an array of low tables, which he
described as "an informal group, fascinating… a coffee table calmly conservative… a
cocktail table in black ebony that is quite irresistible… tops that bravely defy cigarettes,
alcohol and water".

Russel Wright photographed his own Manhattan apartment interiors to showcase his
design vision, even if none of the pieces in the settings were meant to be mass-produced
like his American Modern dinnerware and furnishings. At the centre of his living room in
the Concord Apartments, East 40th Street, circa 1937, was a low circular table in black
vitrolite, raised on tubular steel legs, on which he placed glassware and bottles, and
which revolved to serve each guest. The table was surrounded by other Bauhaus-inspired
furniture, yet the room was warmed by the animal-skin rug and landscape paintings on
the wall. Here, the table was clearly depicted as the centre of the room's spatial and
entertainment axis.

15. Russel Wright
revolving coffee table, circa 1934

16. Frederick Kiesler
table with lamp from the Mergentine interior, 1935

Frederick Kiesler
drawing for furniture, 1935
Placed on the central table is a
lamp that appears to be
inspired by Poul Henningsen's
PH series. The actual table
incorporates its own surreal
light source.

An avant-garde breakthrough was achieved for coffee tables in 1935 by Frederick Kiesler. In a design for a Manhattan apartment, Kiesler placed at the centre of the living room a circular glass-topped tubular steel table, clearly descended from Breuer, yet giving off its own theatrical vibe in being tricked up with wheels and a floodlight. One could chalk this up as a strange fruit of Kiesler's overactive imagination (in a ten year period he had joined the De Stijl group, collaborated with the Constructivists and the Surrealists including his chess partner Marcel Duchamp, helped found AUDAC and ran a design laboratory at Columbia University). But in the foreground of a single sketch that predates the Manhattan apartment was something altogether more radical. To the side of one lounge chair was a pair of amoebic "nested coffee tables". Design conventions had been shattered. It was a coffee table that sounded the clarion call for the age of biomorphism. Kiesler's design was the product of his mystifying teachings in 'biotechnique' at Columbia. Inspired by Surrealism, Kiesler wasn't reacting so much to the Machine Age propaganda fomented by streamlining as he was developing the concept that indeterminate, poetic shapes can serve rational, functional considerations.

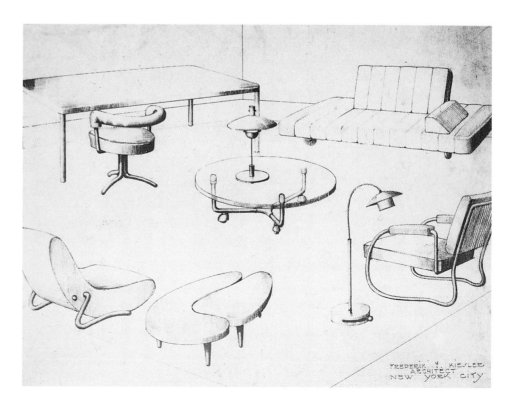

Gilbert Rohde
advertisement in the Herman Miller Fall 1940 Supplement

48

At the same time, in England, Marcel Breuer was experimenting with bending wood under steam pressure, developing a line of furniture for Isokon. His rectangular coffee table, with its tentacle legs cut from the same plywood sheet as the top, was both technologically innovative and inspired by Surrealism. When Breuer moved to America in 1937, his plywood experiments grew more biomorphic, as seen in his coffee tables for the Frank House in Pittsburgh.

Organic shapes began creeping into furniture designs everywhere. A glass coffee table from the late 1930s of unknown origin, but now in the collection of the Metropolitan Museum of Art in New York, illustrates the tentative steps being taken by even anonymous designers to keep up with the new trend. At the same time, it must be remembered that the term "coffee table", which we have been using here somewhat liberally in

charting its development in the 1930s, was, of course, not always being used at the time by designers. But then it was used, and it was used everywhere. The transitional season seems to have been 1939-1940. The perfect example of this change in nomenclature was the 1940 Herman Miller catalogue, featuring the designs of Gilbert Rohde. When it was published, the catalogue clearly focused on models that were already in production, thus probably dating in concept to 1939 and earlier. A two-page spread entitled "Luxury Group of Occasional Tables" featured Rohde's designs in Lucite, a material which was quickly replacing glass as the material of the moment. Every one of these 'occasional tables' is in fact a coffee table to our eyes, and most remain quite orthodox in their shape, with rectangular and circular glass tops supported by Lucite legs.

But at the back of the catalogue is the "Fall 1940 Supplement". Rohde had

been busy. He introduced his Paldao line of tables as "the answer to the demand for bigger and better Coffee Tables". The materials and construction were top-drawer, with paldao walnut edges, acacia burl-wood tops, leather-wrapped legs, and finishes that included mink and sable. Three of the five tables were organic in shape. Not too radical in their form, but the new look was obvious. And everywhere you read, the titles had changed. "Occasional" had been replaced by "Coffee".

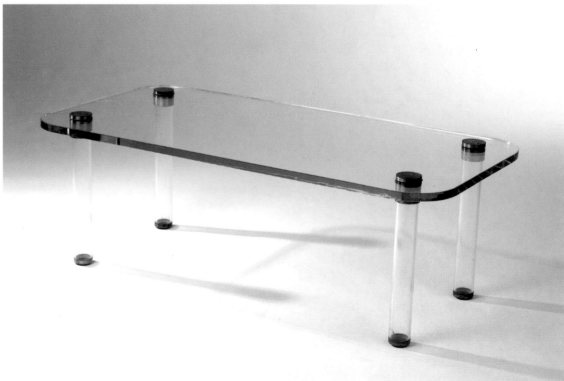

Marcel Breuer and Walter Gropius
the Frank house, Pittsburgh, PA, 1939

Marcel Breuer
living room at Heals, London, April 1936

Perhaps one of the best period books that illustrates the increased frequency in the role (and accepted naming) of the coffee table is Design of Modern Interiors by James and Katherine Morrow Ford, published in 1942. Meant as a shelter guide to architects and interior designers, Ford and Ford collected the best interiors from Cape Cod to Beverly Hills, and the array of coffee table forms is staggering. As Ford and Ford write in their introduction, "The rigid formalities and 'correct' social groupings about a center table of a former era give way to the informalities of the cocktail, tea or buffet party." Throughout the book are tentative organic shapes by architects who have today fallen into obscurity, such as "The freeform coffee table covered in rawhide" by the designer Ann Hatfield for a family room in New Jersey. On other pages, we see icons in the history of design casually scattered about, such as Breuer's seminal biomorphic shapes, for the

Frank house in Pittsburgh and Richard Neutra's Camel table pictured in several of his interiors, which "can be raised to dining height or lowered to tea table height by a 20 second manipulation", but is photographed every time as a coffee table in front of a sofa.

Standard rectangular coffee tables were everywhere too, clearly named as such, and comfortably placed in positions that we are familiar with today. On facing pages are sterling examples of the form, one by the Chicago architect Samuel Marx, and one by Paul Frankl. But on page 53, simply put, was the most staggering development in the history of coffee table design, something that drew on the amoebic shapes of Kiesler and Breuer while pushing the envelope even further, a design that would influence much of what we now call "mid-century modern".

In 1939, Isamu Noguchi was commissioned by A Conger Goodyear, the first President of the Museum of Modern Art to create a sculptural table for his residence in Old Westbury, Long Island. As Bruce Altshuler writes, "the primary stress was between utopian ambitions and the need to court wealthy patrons, a tension evident in the circumstances of Noguchi's first table design, a low glass-topped table with articulated rosewood supports. The Goodyear table points towards the biomorphic Surrealism that Noguchi developed more fully in his sculpture of the following decade".
More importantly, this table would serve as the prototype for his IN-50 coffee table of 1947, which has been manufactured by Herman Miller virtually uninterrupted to the present day. This organic masterpiece truly jumpstarted the mid-century modern era, the age of Herman Miller and Knoll's mass produced organic designs. But in 1942, when Ford and Ford first published photos of it for Americans to see, the design world had not yet made the complete transition. The conservative style of the authors almost hides their excitement: "Noguchi table is of movable sections of laminated wood, allowing the forms to be re-composed at will; its top is of herculite glass." The table for Goodyear marks a liminal moment in design, a masterpiece that straddles 1930s to 1940s American modernism and Post War mid-century modernism, where organic design reigned supreme.

19. Wolfgang Hoffmann
coffee tables, model no 803, 1934
The brute strength of Hoffmann's
design, with its exposed screws and
double-crossed braces, is an icon
of America's 'Machine Age', and is
the most enduring model of his
tenure at the Howell Company,
1934-1942.

20. Warren McArthur
coffee table, circa 1930s
A classic example of American
Machine Age design, the joinery
construction is proudly
emphasised as an illustration
of the assembly process. The
icy, muted finish of the
anodised aluminium tubes
appealed to the Park Avenue
clients of McArthur.

21. Denham MacLaren
coffee table, 1936

22. Denham MacLaren
sculpture/coffee table, 1936

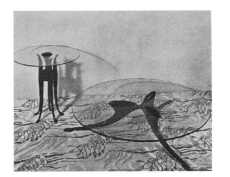

Denham MacLaren
two tables for Duncan Miller, London, 1936
John Duncan Miller was a pioneering
modernist in England in the 1930s. He
published two books: *Interior decorating*,
1937, and *More colour schemes for the
modern home*, 1938, and championed the
avant-garde. MacLaren was at the time
considered a designer of the same caliber
and merit as his continental European
counterparts such as Gray.

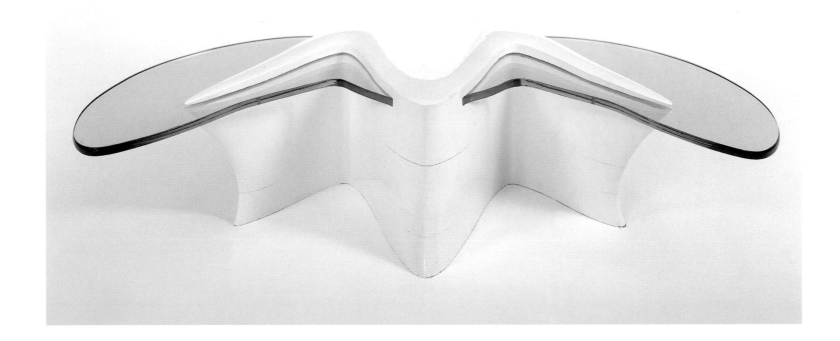

23. Frederick Kiesler
nesting coffee table, 1935-1938
A unique example, originally
designed for Mr and Mrs Martin
Janis.

24. Frederick Kiesler
nesting coffee table, 1935-1938
The earliest masterpiece of the
organic design movement. There
are two examples of this model
known to exist.

25. Gilbert Rohde
no 4188 coffee table, 1940

Gilbert Rohde
Herman Miller advertisement, Fall 1940
"Numbers 4187 and 4186 are first
cousins in a lamp and coffee table,
unconventional in shape but very
dignified and luxurious."

26. Eileen Gray
free-form table, from Tempe à Pailla, circa 1935
As with her table design for Jacques Doucet two
decades earlier, Eileen Gray always seemed to be
ahead of her time. This table dates to as early as
1930, making it a possible predecessor to Kiesler
and Breuer's biomorphic designs. There are four
versions of this design listed in Gray's catalogue
raisonée. She first employed the boiss brulé, or
scorched wood technique in the late teens.

27. Paul Dupré-Lafon
table basse, circa 1930s

28. T H Robsjohn-Gibbings
low table from the Casa Encantada, circa 1937
From the British decorator's most famous
interior in Bel Air, later owned by Conrad
Hilton and abused by Zsa Zsa Gabor.
Robsjohn-Gibbings explored his obsession
with Greek classicism at various points in his
long career. This table dates to his first years
in America, before establishing himself as a
household name as a designer of simplified
biomorphic tables for the masses.

29. Maison Jansen
table basse, circa 1940
The venerated decorating firm of
Jansen continued to rehash the
styles of centuries past, yet
subtly adapted them for the
modern interior.

30. Marcel Breuer
low table, circa 1936
This is part of a group of
designs by Breuer for the Isokon
furniture company, set up by
Jack Pritchard in England in
1936.

Marcel Breuer
cut-out plywood sofa
and coffee table, circa 1939

31. Kaare Klimt
low table, circa 1930s

62

32. Charlotte Perriand
low table, circa 1939
Designed just prior to Perriand's
historic stay in Japan during
World War Two, this table's
design foreshadows her
exploration of the "Synthese des
Arts" between Eastern and
Western cultures.

33. Tommi Parzinger
coffee table, 1939
Only a few years after
immigrating to New York,
Parzinger exhibited this unique
table at Rena Rosenthal's
interior design shop. The tribal
carved legs owe a debt to
Legrain, while the overall
French style places it firmly in
the American school of Frank
followers. The pewter top
provides an unusual touch.

35. Marc Du Plantier
table basse, circa 1934
The designs of Du Plantier and
Dupre-Lafon illustrate the
emergence of a new modernism
in the salons of Paris.

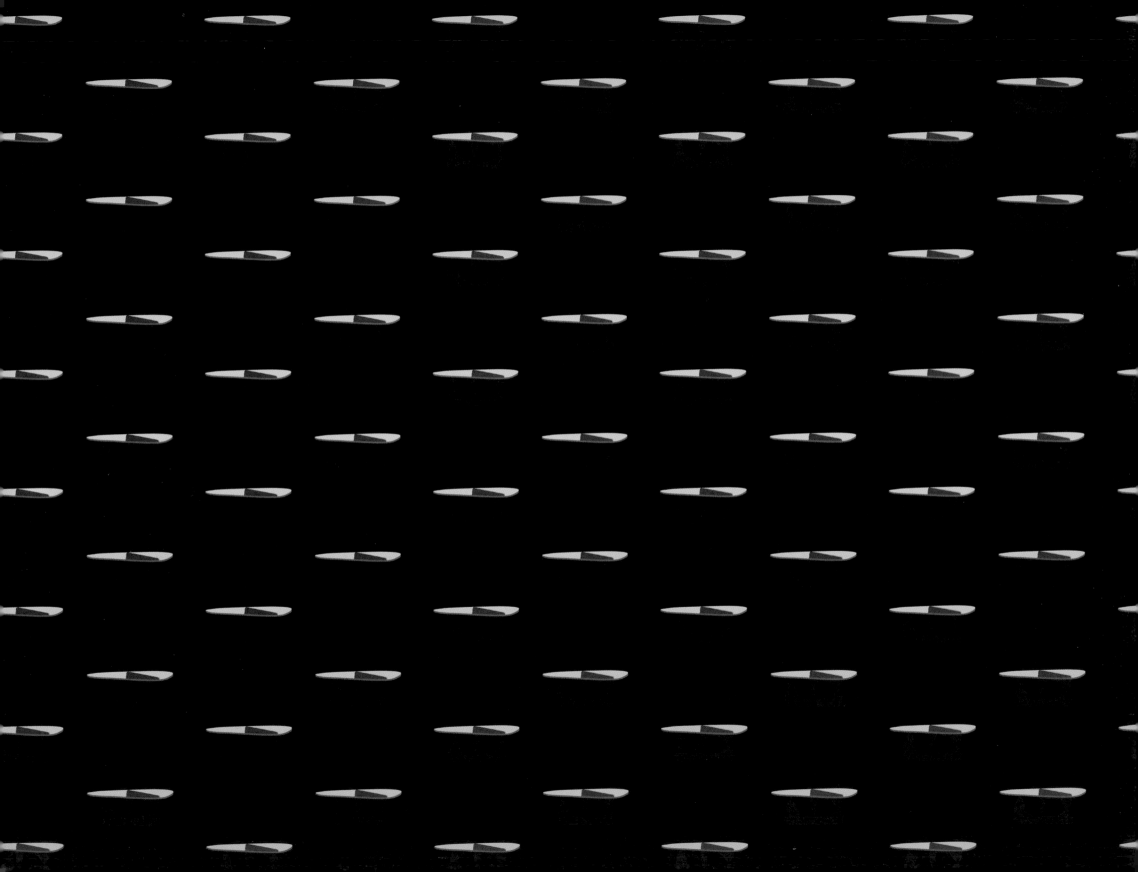

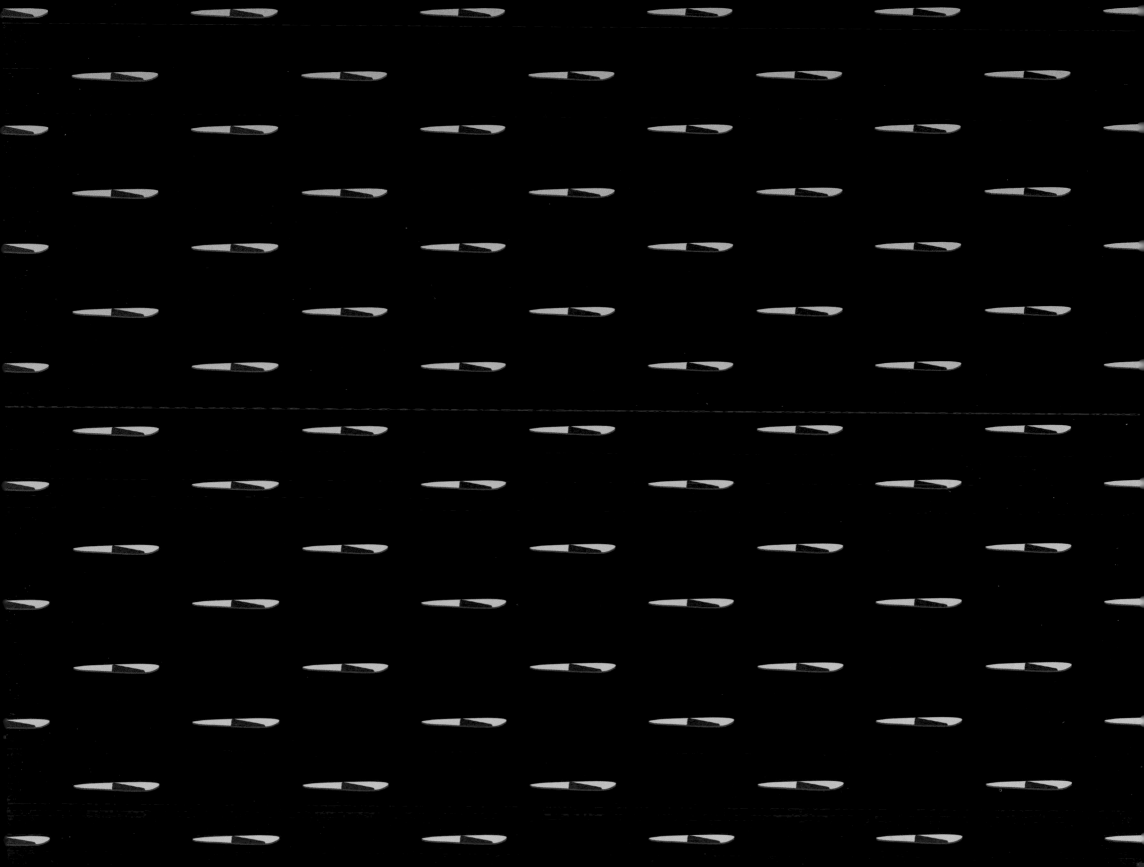

four

mid-century
the coffee table comes of age

During World War Two, with the mass production of furniture largely curtailed, the most important coffee table concepts were produced for private commissions and museum exhibitions. In looking through the catalogues of furniture manufacturers who survived this period, however, the term "coffee table" was completely established in the vocabulary of most design conscious consumers, particularly in America.

It is also clear, given this literature, that the organic and the biomorphic forms reigned supreme. Isamu Noguchi's table for A Conger Goodyear in 1939, the most important private commision of the period, was published in numerous books on interiors during this period, illustrating the sculptural ideal of this new trend. In New York, Frederick Kiesler's Surrealist installation of linoleum and plywood furniture for Peggy Guggenheim's Art of This Century Gallery, would also prove to be highly influential on both artists and designers.

The Organic Design in Home Furnishings Competition, held at the Museum of Modern Art, in 1941, launched the careers of Charles Eames and Eero Saarinen. While the emphasis of their award-winning entries was on seating and modular furnishings, they did exhibit a "low coffee table," probably manufactured for the occasion by Heywood-Wakefield. This sculptural three-legged design was in the tradition of bent plywood—the ideal low-cost modernist material—as seen in the 1930s in the work of Alvar Aalto and in the Isokon designs of Marcel Breuer, both of whom served on the jury of the competition. Another "freeform coffee table" was featured as part of the prize-winning entry for a one bedroom apartment submitted by Martin Craig and Anne Hatfield, and was available for sale at Bloomingdale's Department Store. Low cost "good design for everyone" in organic shapes would prove to be the barometer for the decade.

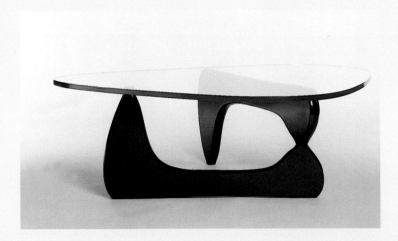

In August 1942, an advertisement appeared in Interiors Magazine for Hans Knoll
Furniture. Promoting the second season of furniture manufactured by the fledgling
company, the centrepiece of the living room illustration was the Cloud Cocktail Table,
model 600, designed by Jens Risom, a young Danish freelancer who had moved to New
York a few years earlier. Although this line of furniture was not terribly successful, and
the table has rarely been seen since (Risom soon left the firm to serve in the army; when
he returned in 1945, Florence Schust had married Hans and taken over as chief designer)
the precedent was set: a future powerhouse of mid-century modern furniture
manufacturing—soon to become known as Knoll Associates—would make the organic
coffee table a mainstay of their lines for the next decade, producing examples by
Alexander Girard, Abel Sorenson and Florence Knoll.

HANS KNOLL FURNITURE
SHOWROOM · 601 MADISON AVENUE · NEW YORK · PLAZA 3-3636

"CHERRY WOOD" LINE BY JENS RISOM

SPECIAL DESIGNS MADE TO ORDER

SPECIALIZING IN FURNITURE CONTRACTS

CATALOGUE UPON REQUEST

INTERIORS

One mass produced biomorphic coffee table made during this period that did enjoy successful sales was a fey glass and blondewood number designed by T H Robsjohn-Gibbings for Widdicomb in 1942. Robsjohn-Gibbings, an English designer, decorator and onetime antique furniture dealer, emigrated to the United States in the mid-1930s. He quickly found work as a decorator to the stars and socialites, from Park Avenue to Beverly Hills. Emphasising a 'timeless' look that incorporated clean lines and trendy pastiches of modernism, he adapted this for the masses in his Widdicomb furniture line. His bemused, provocative voice appeared in satirical essays on decorating and culture and managed to infuriate antique lovers and avant-garde modernists alike in such bestsellers as "Good Bye, Mr Chippendale", 1944, and "Homes of the Brave", 1954.

In the late 1930s Robsjohn-Gibbings' coffee table designs were strictly rectangular takes on Neo-Classicism. But in 1942, after being personally shown a model of the Goodyear table by Noguchi, Robsjohn-Gibbings rushed into production his own version, taking advantage of wartime circumstance—Noguchi had volunteered at a relocation camp for Japanese-Americans during the war years, and was unable to refine what he viewed as not just a unique commission, but also a prototype for mass production. Robsjohn-Gibbings' resulting "freeform coffee table" for Widdicomb infuriated Noguchi, who accused the Englishman of stealing his design.

No matter, however. As Martin Eidelberg writes "once the war was over, and designers could let loose their imaginations, the creative potential of Biomorphism was unleashed". And in 1947, reportedly influenced by the George Nelson essay

36. T H Robsjohn Gibbings
coffee table, 1943

"How to Make a Table", Noguchi achieved catharsis by releasing his own mass produced version of his prototype. The IN-50 table for Herman Miller, featured a pair of wooden elements, one flipped 180 degrees and pinned to the other, and a glass top that seemed to achieve a perfection of freeform improvisation. One critic wrote: "rarely found in such translation of 'fine' art are the almost organic unity and the logic of the structure of the whole, compromising neither with art nor utility". Perhaps the best-selling modernist coffee table of all time, in near-continuous production by Herman Miller since its release, the zenith of the style had now been achieved. Robsjohn-Gibbings did manage to develop his own original organic coffee table design in the early 1950s, when he looked to the American desert as inspiration for his tiered Mesa coffee table, also produced by Widdicomb. But his role as Noguchi's nemesis remains an interesting footnote in coffee table lore, and shows the two designers' own awareness that coffee tables shaped like kidneys were sure best-sellers.

In Paris, the interior designer Jean Royère was the undisputed champion of the amoeba-shaped table basse. From 1945 until 1960 Royère designed countless models for clients in France, Lebanon and South America. Perhaps his definitive contribution to the genre was the Flaque marquetry table, which appears in numerous period photographs and watercolours in his archive at the Musée des Arts décoratifs. In general, the French continued to design their living spaces without employing coffee tables, but Royère, whose designs frequently appeared in international publications, seemed to thrive on blending the French decorating tradition with American influences, both in the shapes of his work as well as in their arrangement.

In Italy, the architect and designer Carlo Mollino contributed a supercharged eroticism to coffee table design as part of his "Turinese organic" style. The extremes to which Mollino pursued his many passions, from photography to butterfly collecting, certainly marked him as a twentieth century Renaissance man. When Mollino embraced a new hobby he did so with the obsessive fervour of an Olympian. Mollino didn't just design racing cars, he was the winning driver at Le Mans in 1954. He didn't just shoot erotic photographs of his mistresses and models, he styled their hair, designed their lingerie and shoes, and used their poses as inspirations for his anthropomorphic chairs and tables. In an undated drawing of the back of a model, he traced the outlines of her form and used it for the glass top of a coffee table design. Ultimately, Mollino designed several variations on this theme for various interiors, from the famed "Arabesque" to a version

Lenore Fini
study of Reclining Female, circa 1950
The traced outline is by Carlo Mollino
and was used as a template for glass
tops on tables including the
Arabesque.

retailed in America by Singer.
The rise of Post War Italian design meant that
numerous coffee tables were concieved in Milan and
Turin, and not just in the organic style. Singer & Sons
opened a retail shop in New York, featuring circular
and rectilinear coffee tables by Gio Ponti, Ico Parisi,
Carlo di Carli and Mollino. Fontana Arte
manufactured designs by Ponti and Pietro Chiesa,
arguably, the first practioners of a new mid-century
modern genre—the decorative coffee table top.
Whether in a modernist or historicist vein, it seemed
natural for these designers to take the classic
rectangular shape and add ceramics, mosaics or
other types of media to the coffee tables' top. The
sculptor Mirko Balsadella's unique coffee tables were
typical of the new look: a simple modernist base with
a glass top painted by hand with a mixture of plaster
and pigmented marble dust. Piero Fornasetti
decorated tables designed by Ponti with surrealist
trompe l'oeil lithographs. In America, this new
approach was quickly adopted by New York-based
interior designers who also produced affordable
examples for the fly-over states through their
furniture lines. Edward Wormley, influenced by his
friend Edgar Kaufmann, (the powerful Museum of
Modern Art curator, who was busy collecting Art
Nouveau works that he considered 'proto-Modern' for

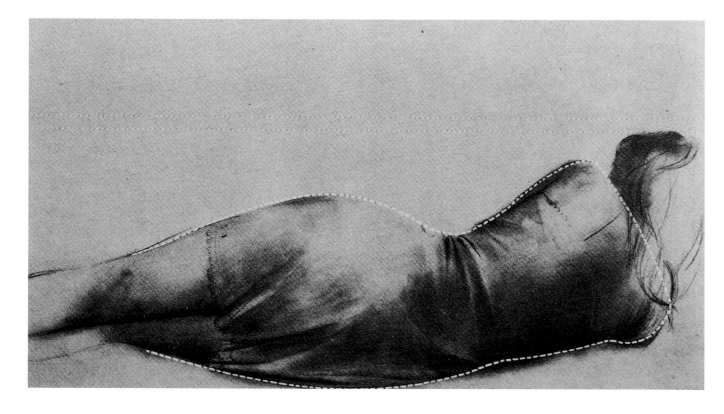

House Beautiful, July 1958
A spectacular regional
interpretation of Noguchi's
masterpiece. The architect here
used driftwood and what appears
to be an actual glass top from
the IN-50 for a residence in
Hawaii.

37. Poul Kjærholm
PK-61, 1956

76

the Museum's collection), began
adding salvaged 50 year old
iridescent tiles by Tiffany Studios to
his table top designs for Dunbar.
Later, he collaborated with the
ceramicists Gertrude and Otto Natzler
on similar decorations.

But as in the previous decade in
America, when the International Style
had eventually prevailed over
streamlining as the best path towards
Good Design Utopia, it was inevitable
that those critics who had been
briefly under the Surrealist spell of
biomorphicism would return to the
temple of Mies. Starting in the early
1950s, there were the beginnings of a
backlash. The influential Kaufmann
wisecracked in a 1952 essay that the
biomorphic coffee table had become
an object of kitsch. And while the
organic and 'atomic' shapes were
prevalent in all forms of furniture,
the coffee table seemed uniquely
suited for the medium, and thus was
ultimately susceptible to cliché.

By this time, there were nearly a
dozen terms employed by designers to
describe their organic shaped tables,
from "amoeba" to "cloud-form".
Browsing through the pages of the
Decorative Art yearbooks from
1950-1955, there were numerous such
examples made in America (Robsjohn-
Gibbings, Wormley, the aging Paul
Frankl and a youngster named
Vladimir Kagan were all stars) and in
England, where "nimbus" and
"boomerang" tables were retailed by
such firms as H Morris and Co Ltd of
Glasgow and Liberty of London. In
California, the rattan furniture craze
was a boon for biomorphism.
Harvested and manufactured in the
Philippines, Los Angeles firms
including Tropical Sun Rattan and
Ritts Co. (founded by Herb Ritts Sr,
father of the famed fashion
photographer) produced low-cost
Formica-topped examples for every
setting, from tract housing in Phoenix
to rumpus rooms in the San Fernando
Valley.

But such regionalism is usually the
last gasp of a style, and by 1955 the
International Style's ornery cousin
Good Design had prevailed. Perhaps
the most important sign of a shift in
taste was Knoll's reissue of Mies'
table from the Barcelona Pavilion,
renamed the Barcelona Coffee Table,
which quickly became a best-seller.
Along with Florence Knoll's own
Parallel Bars design and the PK61
table designed by Poul Kjaerholm, the
new look was minimalist and
architectonic. These three table
designs, along with their many look-
alikes, would become the first
generation of models on which coffee
table books would be placed—along
with the coffee, cocktails, ashtrays
and plants. Although the next decade
would reverberate with bright colours,
plastics, illuminations and even a
brief resurgence of the biomorphic, it
would be these late designs of the
1950s that would continue to spawn
imitators through to the end of the
century.

living room in Peter Moro's apartment,
London, circa 1960
Featuring furniture by Robin Day—at the
centre is the Cheyne table.

38. Isamu Noguchi
IN-50, 1947
Examples in blondewood
(birch or walnut) were produced
in more limited editions than
the ebonised versions.

39. Abel Sorensen
coffee table, 1948

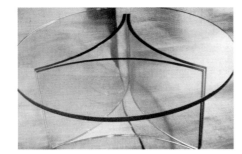

40. Piero Chiesa
coffee tables, circa 1957
produced by Fontana Arte,
retailed in America by Singer & Sons

Samuel Marx
The Joseph Block Residence,
Chicago, IL, 1948

41. Samuel Marx
coffee table, circa 1948
Marx produced this mirrored
table for several of his
Midwestern clients. Its
expanded size illustrates a
growing trend towards using the
coffee table for the display of
books, objects and plants.

80

Samuel Marx
The Joseph Block residence

42. Samuel Marx
book table, 1948
A unique design, perhaps the
most stunning and early
example of what became a
1950s trend: the addition of
shelving to coffee table designs
to accommodate books and
magazines.

43. Edward Wormley
coffee table from the Janus Collection, 1956

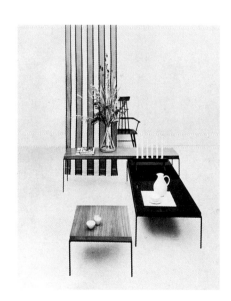

47. Charles and Ray Eames
Three-Legged Tray Table, 1945
This extraordinary prototype was built
by the Eames office and the Molded
Plywood Division of their firm Evans.
It is believed that two or three of this
model were made, which was
subsequently exhibited in late 1945
and 1946 in New York at the Barclay
Hotel, the Architectural League, and
the seminal show New Furniture
designed by Charles Eames at the
Museum of Modern Art.

48. Charles and Ray Eames
OTWs (Occasional Table Wood), 1946
Perhaps this model illustrates best
the Eames' contributions to the
history of bent plywood design. The
table's effortless curves make it
the perfect companion to the
Eames' iconic LCWs.

a Herman Miller advertising shot for moulded plywood furniture by Charles and Ray Eames, circa 1948

49. Charles and Ray Eames
CTW (Coffee Table Wood), 1946

Jean Royère
Hall d'un chalet à Megève, 1953-1956
pencil and gouache on Canson paper

50. Jean Prouvé
low tables, circa 1950s
These models, which were
produced in several different
variants, are often referred to
as the African tables.

90

51. Charlotte Perriand and Jean Prouvé
free-form tables, circa 1953
Although squabbles continue to this
day amongst academics, family
members, dealers and collectors, it is
generally agreed that the varying tops
of these tables were designed by
Perriand, while the powerful iron
supports are by Prouvé, whose firm
also manufactured the entire piece.

52. George Nelson Associates
coffee table, model no 4696, 1949
"For use when a free shape is
desired", this table disappeared
from the Herman Miller catalogues
after 1950. Only a few examples of
the model are known to exist.

53. Charles and Ray Eames
ETR (Elliptical Table Rod Base), 1950
Inspired by the Californian waves,
sun and sand, the 'surfboard' table
illustrates the Eames' regionalist
flair and creative use of popular
culture in their designs.

Isamu Kenmochi
coffee table, circa 1955

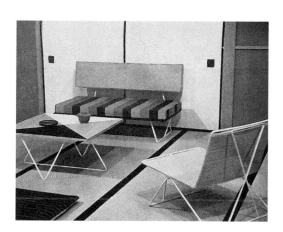

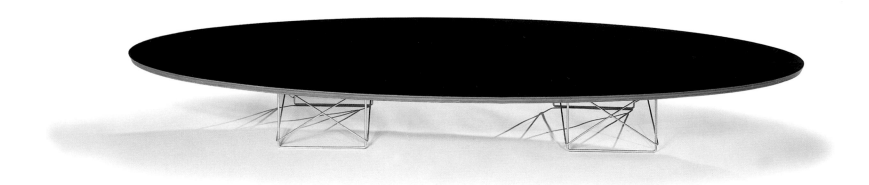

55. Tapio Wirkkala
coffee table, 1958

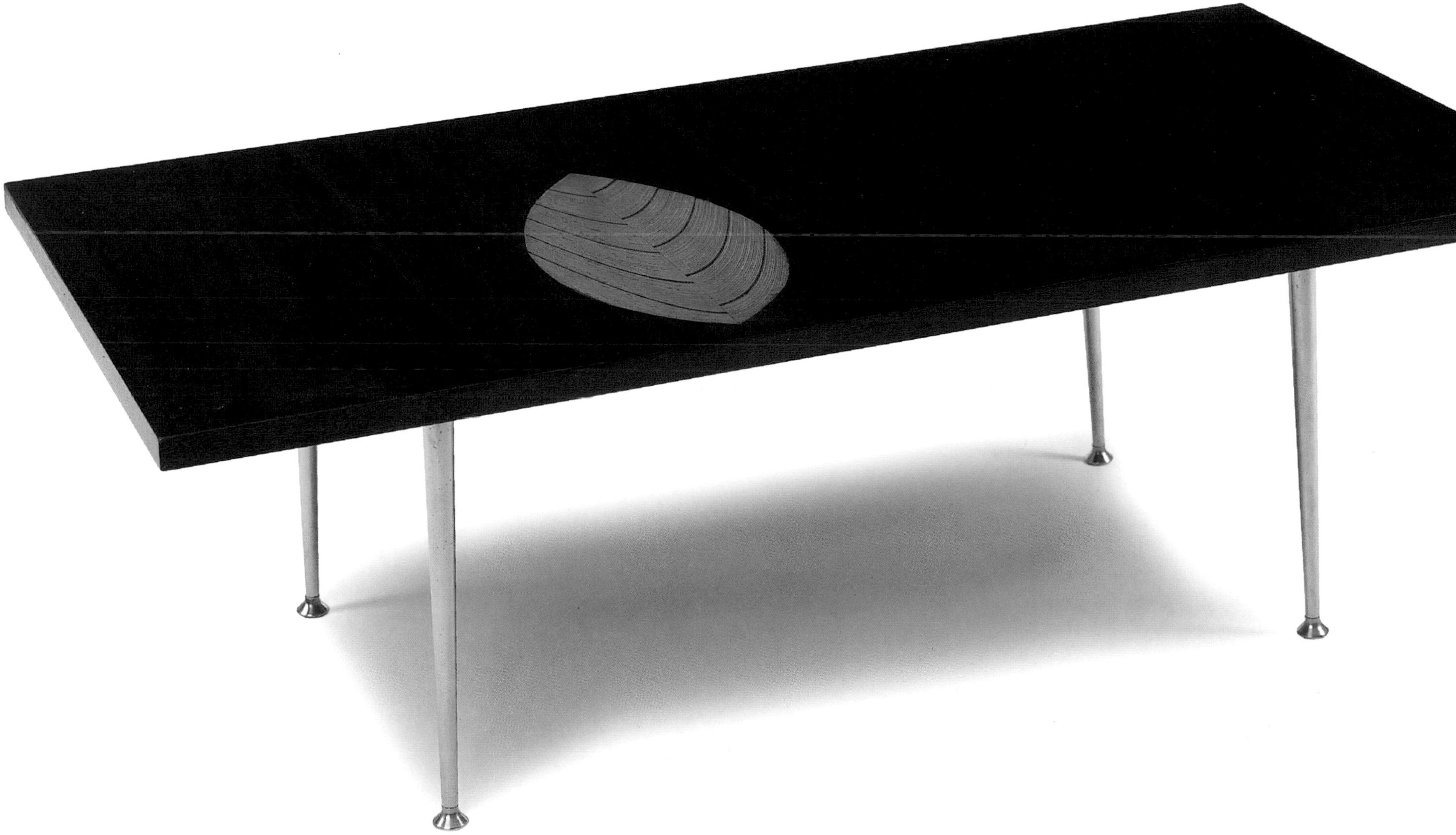

56. unknown American designer
coffee table, circa 1950s
Believed to have been
manufactured by the American
firm Lane, this table frequently
appears on the market.
Graceful and whimsical at the
same time, it epitomises the
full flowering of the biomorphic
in mid-century America.

57. William 'Billy' Haines
Mesa Table, 1955
The Los Angeles based decorator
did only a handful of furniture
models that he reproduced for
more than one client, including
this table, where he appears to
have channeled Noguchi via
Robsjohn-Gibbings.

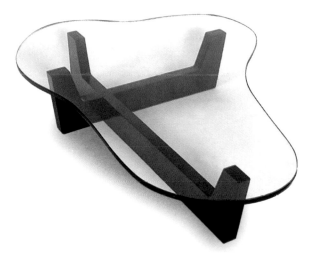

58. Paul Frankl
coffee table, circa 1950s
After Frankl moved to California in the 1930s, his furniture designs became less symbolic, less propogandistic, and more suited for the Los Angeles estates that he decorated. He also enjoyed several successful mass-productions of his designs by midwestern furniture companies, including Johnson. There are several variations of this organic cork-topped table, all reproduced in the Studio Yearbooks of the 1950s.

59. Edward Wormley
coffee table, model 5307, circa 1950s

60. T H Robsjohn-Gibbings
Mesa coffee table, 1950s
Inspired by the contours of the
southwestern desert, the Mesa is
arguably Robsjohn-Gibbings'
finest design. Less derivitive
than his earlier organic models,
and indescribably chic.

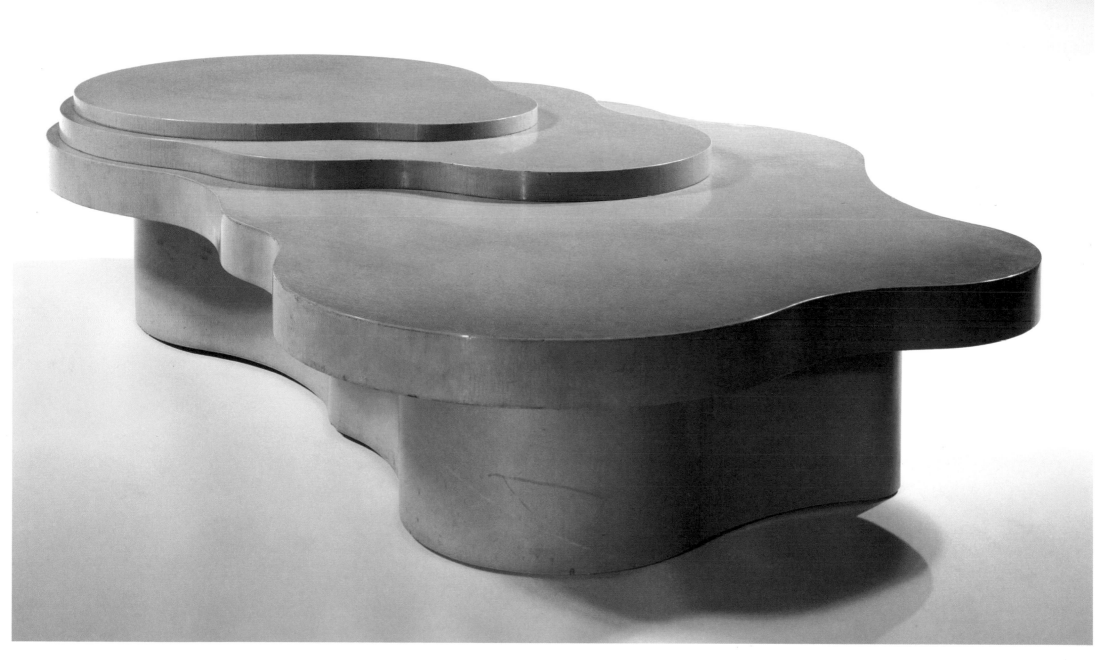

61. Vladimir Kagan
coffee table, circa 1950s

62. Gio Ponti
coffee table, 1953-1954

Fontana Arte
coffee table, circa 1950s

Carlo Mollino
coffee table with magazine shelf from Casa M1, 1944

Carlo Mollino
coffee table from Casa M1, 1944

Jacques Adnet
Hunting lodge, published in 1952,
in Decor et Amenagement
de la Maison. The rare table is by
the French sculptor and designer
Alexandre Noll.

64. Jacques Adnet and Hermès
coffee table, circa 1950
These tables were easily found
in the Paris flea markets until
several years ago. French
decorators always employed
such leather-wrapped, faux-
bamboo designs in country
houses, but recently they have
become faddish in New York City
interiors.

65: Charlotte Perriand
low table, 1941
from the exhibition "Tradition
Selection Creation", held at the
Takeshimaya Department Stores in
Tokyo and Osaska, March-May 1941.

66. Charlotte Perriand
table basse, 1954

67. George Nakashima
coffee table, model no 10, 1946
The earliest Nakashima designs
for Knoll were his most severe
and modernist. It took another
decade for the New Hope
woodworker to develop his
organic style.

68. Greta Magnusson Grossman
coffee tables, circa 1952
Southern California attracted an
abundance of self-made, self-taught
architects and designers from
around the globe, and the Swedish-
born Grossman found success as
both an industrial designer and an
architect. Her graceful series of
table designs for Glenn of California
epitomise the organic movement.

71. T H Robsjohn-Gibbings
coffee table, circa 1950
In the centre of the rectangular
top is a magazine rack.

Allan Gould
coffee table, 1950s

Poul Kjærholm
PK-61, 1956
The model was available in
three tops – glass, rolled
marble and black slate.

72. Dan Johnson
prototype coffee table, model B-100, 1958
Although not as celebrated as his Gazelle
series of chairs, this travertine and steel
prototype served as the basis for
Johnson's first line of cocktail tables.
Probably built in Italy, where Johnson
resided in the late 1950s.

73. Arne Jacobsen
coffee table, 1958

74. Georg Jensen
coffee table, circa 1960

76. Julio Katinsky
coffee table, 1951-1958
One of São Paulo's most
important architects, Katinsky
designed furniture for the
Brazilian firm L'Atlelier, which
as their name suggests,
exported to the European market.

77. Edgar Bartolucci and Robert Cato
coffee table, circa 1954
Bartolucci teamed up with graphic
designer Robert Cato, a fellow
Chicago Institute of Design alumnus,
to create a small series of tables,
with its five interchangeable
coloured panels, each painted a
solid colour on one side and with
Cato's abstract designs on the other.

78. Russel Wright
Trayble, 1950
Perhaps the root of all evil. This best-seller encouraged Americans to eat their TV dinners directly in front of the tube. It was also meant to be used as an outdoor patio table.

Richard Neutra
Camel table, 1961
upright position

Richard Neutra
Camel Table in Ward House,
North Hollywood, CA, 1940

79. Richard Neutra
Camel table from the Cytron
House, circa 1961
low position

80. Paul László
coffee table, circa 1958
Yet another funky table from
Southern California by a
European transplant. This table
also comes with wheels, which
makes it look rather like a
mortuary table. László
collaborated with the sculptor
F F Kern on the ebonized wood
bases of these custom-built
tables. He also designed
numerous mass-produced coffee
tables for Glenn of California.

Paul László
Another example of the model in
the residence of Mr and Mrs
Julian M saks, Beverly Hills, CA

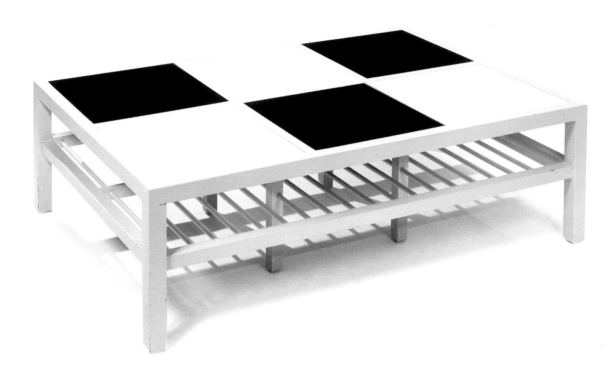

82. Edward Wormley
refectory coffee table, model no 5427, circa 1950s

photograph from the 1956
Dunbar catalogue—the pastoral
bliss of Eisenhower-era
suburbia

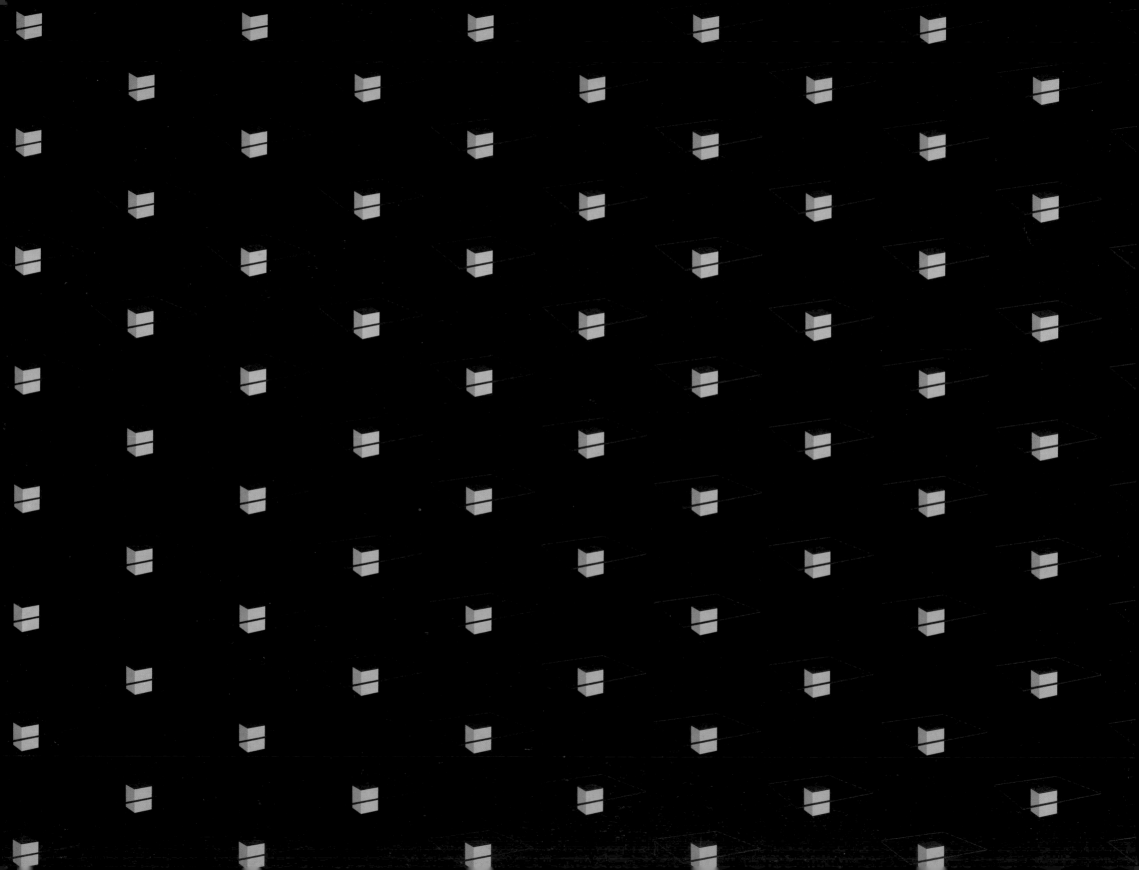

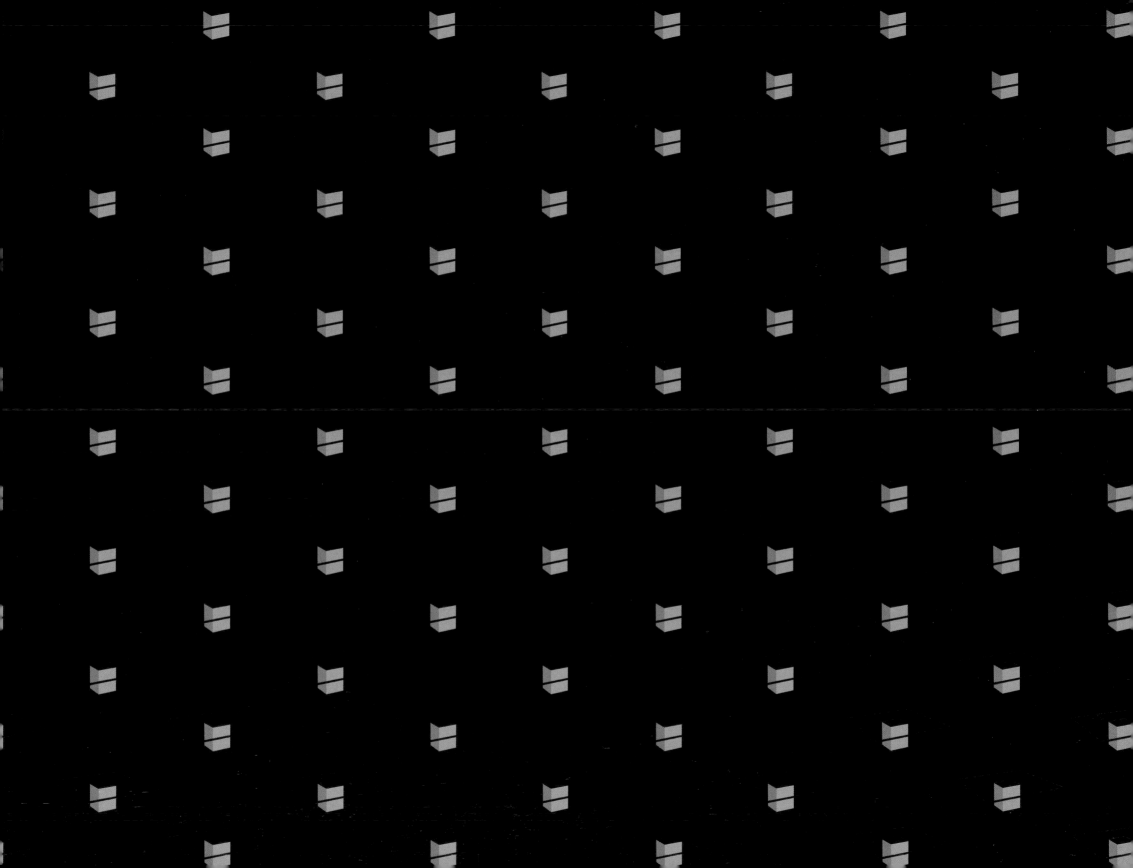

five

from pop to crisis point

When it came to domestic interiors, the early 1960s were really quite tame. The living room as depicted in contemporary periodicals was a sleepy lullaby, as decorators continued to subscribe to the twin tenants of "Good Design" and the International Style.

In America, the only radical and liminal form that bridged mid-century modernism and the pop era were the omnipresent tulip tables of Eero Saarinen, their varying sizes and surfaces sprouting, like weeds, in both public and private spaces. Otherwise, the typical living room as depicted in House and Garden could be described in two words:

Wormley and Dunbar. By 1965, Edward Wormley had probably designed over 100 coffee tables, and the vignettes of the Dunbar catalogue exhibited his passions for Scandinavian design and the styles of previous centuries, from the Ming Dynasty to Richard Riemerschmid. But the purity of these influences had been traded for a comfy Midwestern outlook.

A noticeable blandness was settling in, and his coffee tables were representative of the gradual decline in new ideas. In England, too, the cost-conscious and curator-approved furniture of Robin and Lucienne Day seemed increasingly oppressive, as 'Swinging London' began to influence a wider swath of culture.

85. Minoru Yamasaki
coffee table, circa 1972
Yamasaki, the architect of the World Trade
Center, designed this coffee table and used
it in various Michigan homes. The table
represents the ideals of the International
Style and was the perfect centre piece for
Girard's "Conversation Pits".

David Hemmings and Vanessa
Redgrave during the filming of
Blow-Up, 1966.

People began renouncing the 1950s suburban slumber in favour of a
more utopian, ideal way of living. In America, there had already been
experiments in creating intimacy in the living room, as seen in the
"Conversation Pits" of Alexander Girard. In locales as diverse as
suburban Michigan and Santa Fe, Girard framed his sunken "Pits" with
wrap-around sofas enlivened with his trademark pop fabrics. At the
centre, often in front of a fire, was a low slab that served as the coffee
table, where the fondue pot and brandy decanter could be placed or
passed. The emphasis was on bringing people closer together, within
touching distance of each other. It was warmer and more informal.

Pierre Paulin
table 877, circa 1960s
Pictured here Pierre Perigault's
showroom in Paris.

86. Roldofo Bonetto
Quattroquarti, circa 1960s
The table comprises four quarter
sections which can be added to
and stacked on, creating
shelving or linking to form a
wave pattern.

And then, as bongs replaced coffee, as the counter-culture moved into its heyday,
the intimacy of the Conversation Pit spread throughout the entire living area. In
London, swinging socialites flocked to the Sloane Square shop of Baron Albrizzi,
whose signature piece was the Floating Drinks Table, a bright pink or green Lucite
slab, barely 12 inches off the ground. The seat height of living room chairs
became so close to the floor that they were often discarded for the bean-bag or
pillow—or for inflatable furniture by firms such as Quasar. The coffee table
followed suit, sometimes being discarded altogether. The emphasis was on laid
back and mellow. Just as pop artists grew their hair and flirted with censors on
the Ed Sullivan Show, designers were eager to escape the bourgeois living room
in the International Style, as well as the lingering doctrines of Good Design.
Interior design, whether it became highly politicised, as it did in Milan, or more
indicative of the drug culture as seen in various room environments in several
countries, was increasingly so removed from the previous decade's domesticity
that the coffee table was just one of several furniture forms to become irrelevant.

In fact, the spirit of the pop and radical movements didn't fit neatly into a decade but spanned the mid-60s to early 70s—the "Age of Aquarius"—psychedelia, sexual liberation, futuristic domestic environments, pop and political activism. Disposable culture spawned 'throw away' furniture, as designers experimented in laminated paper and cardboard such as Peter Murdoch's These Things—a group comprising chair, table and stool—with low production costs making them perfect for the mass market. Frank Gehry's Easy Edges line was shown in an all-cardboard crash pad at Bloomingdale's in New York, with the underlying theme being one of transience and impermanence. The home also became the "living unit" with young English architects, such as Max Clendinning, turning their attention to furniture design, creating ultra modern interiors within the framework of Georgian and Victorian homes—"the result: cool pop on a nineteenth century backcloth". A new generation of home buyers were not aspiring to their parents idea of the living room, instead they were remodelling it.

These were truly new times for the coffee table and the magazines that came to rest on it. Perhaps the magazine *Nova* best epitomised the mood of the time. Until *Nova* "women's magazines had traditionally been coy about one huge area of women's lives—sex. *Nova* was the first (magazine) to cover the concerns that were also the issues of female liberation—orgasm, contraception, abortion, marriage, childbirth, parenthood, and how to get men, how to keep them and how to enjoy them. This of course appealed to men's curiosity too... not least because the women in the magazine were beautiful and the photography of fashion was often anarchically erotic." If the liberated home had copies of *Nova* and the *Whole Earth Catalogue* lying on the coffee table, there were many that also

Jill Kennington and friend model the silver 'spacey' look for *Nova*, September 1966. In the foreground is William Plunkett's Selsdon coffee table.

88. Angelo Mangiarotti
coffee table, 1959
This is the earliest of many
coffee tables in marble
designed by Mangiarotti in the
1960s-1970s.

138

included *Playboy*, with its famous
motto "Entertainment for Men". These
sexually explicit magazines, along
with the increased popularity in
fashion photography, spawned the
genre of the coffee table book.
Plastic was the new material of the
pop era coffee table. It apotheosised
the innovation in materials and
processes of the time, being a product
capable of realising a designer's most
dynamic aspirations. Importantly, for
the new anti-establishment, yet elitist
consumer of the day, it was a material
that was cheap and accessible.
Injection moulded ABS plastic
(acrylonitrile, butadiene and styrene)
coffee tables rolled off the assembly
lines of European factories in a
rainbow of colours. Today's consumer
might find the forms to be cheap and
cartoonish, better suited for children
than adults. However, such iconic
tables as the Rochchetto by Achille and
Piero Giacomo Castiglion, the
Cantarelli by Eero Aarnio, and a
plethora of designs by Vico Magistretti

Living room by British architect and designer Max Clendinning, 1966-1967. Clendinning's home in Canonbury, London was profiled in the 1966-1967 Decorative Art Studio Yearbook.

Joe Colombo
Central living block of the
"Wohenmodell 1969" shown at
the first Visiona exhibition,
1969.

89. Verner Panton
Ilumesa tables, model no 23600, circa 1970

Verner Panton
Room design for the Visiona 2,
exhibition, 1970.

Pierre Paulin
pedestal group, circa 1961-1962

for Artemide were low-cost and liberating, and continued the main duality of form explored by coffee table designers of the previous decades: the organic and the rectangular.

1969 saw the Space Age stepping into our living rooms as TVs broadcast Neil Armstrong and Buzz Aldrin walking on the moon—feeding the imaginations of both designer and consumer. The Visiona and Visiona 2 exhibitions in Cologne, in 1969 and 1970, showcased the ideas of and experiments by designers Joe Colombo and Verner Panton. Their futuristic environments challenged the benchmarks of design and the way designers thought we were to live— Panton literally created a three-dimensional space using vertical "living towers" in projecting how we might sit, as well as live. He was also interested in the harmony and interaction of objects, and the coffee tables he designed for the

Visiona 2, such as the Ilumesa, reflect this; where the coffee table created the placid ambient light as well as a surface.

The interior of the Hilton Hotel in *2001 A Space Odyssey*, with its legendary foyer clustered with Djinn chairs and sofas by Olivier Mourgue, grouped around Saarinen inspired tulip base coffee tables also caused a sensation. Later in the 1970s Luigi Colani took the environment, the user and living unit to extremes with his Pool seating unit, which combined chair, coffee table and carpet all in one.

The other distinct style of the 1960s and 70s was the glass and steel look. Any Ken Adam set design for a Kubrick or Bond film of the day had to have the de rigeur cool clean lines of a glass and chrome coffee table in the foreground, such as William Plunkett's Selsdon table—a modern day interpretation of Mies. Most of these fashionable tables were

designed by interior decorators, rather than the exalted clique of mostly Italian designers whose works were concurrently being exhibited at the European fairs and the Museum of Modern Art in New York. In America, where many of the previous decade's star designers had moved into the lucrative world of office furniture and systems, George Nelson's Catenary line for Herman Miller, 1963, and Warren Platner's Wire group for Knoll, 1966, were the last major series to continue the modernist tradition of the International Style. The subsequent output by the decorating firms tended to be less rigorous and more flamboyant, with the emphasis on surface not form. The venerable House of Jansen in Paris introduced, for the American market, a line of tables in faux-tortoiseshell, steel and glass, designed by Albrizzi and others, Karl Springer dressed up his tables in python, goat and other animal skins, while Neal Small produced a magical assortment of

90. Achille Castiglioni
Rocchetto, 1967
Plastic gave designers a new
colour palette to work with,
including white, orange,
bordeaux and green.

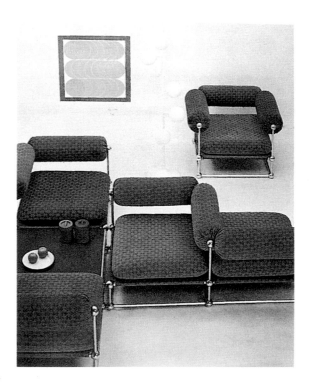

Lucite and acrylic tables for New York's counter-culture socialites. Tables by Guy de Rougemont, John Stefandis and Gabriella Cresi even brought back biomorphism, albeit tempered with the hard edges of the ubiquitous chrome and glass of the period.

Another distinct influence on the coffee table at this time was that of systems furniture. The idea of connecting the coffee table to a chair or sofa became of great interest to designers, as evinced, by Verner Panton's Group S420, where chair and coffee table can be linked together so as to create various seating configurations.

The seminal exhibition in 1972 at the Museum of Modern Art, *Italy: the new domestic landscape*, was to provide an influence that lasted well through the 70s and beyond. Major Italian designers, including Joe Colombo and Ettore Sottsass, created a utopia of systems, reacting to the exhibition's two briefs: to consider design as a method of problem solving and to consider 'counter-design', which underlined the perceived need for a renewal in ideology—both socially and politically—as a way of bringing about change. In these controlled environments furniture items were selected for the flexibility, their use and arrangement, encouraging more informal behaviour in the home.

The Oil Embargo of 1973 (which brought to a standstill the global production of petroleum based plastics), and the world-wide recession of the mid-1970s heralded gloomy times for interior design. The utopian ideals of the most radical Italian designers were muted, although they paved the way for the postmodernist manifestos of Studio Alchemia and Memphis. The coffee table became pedestrian, a fixture to put your feet on, and it would take a new generation of designers in the late 1980s and early 90s to come up with new ideas for the form.

91. Warren Platner
Platner coffee table, circa 1960s

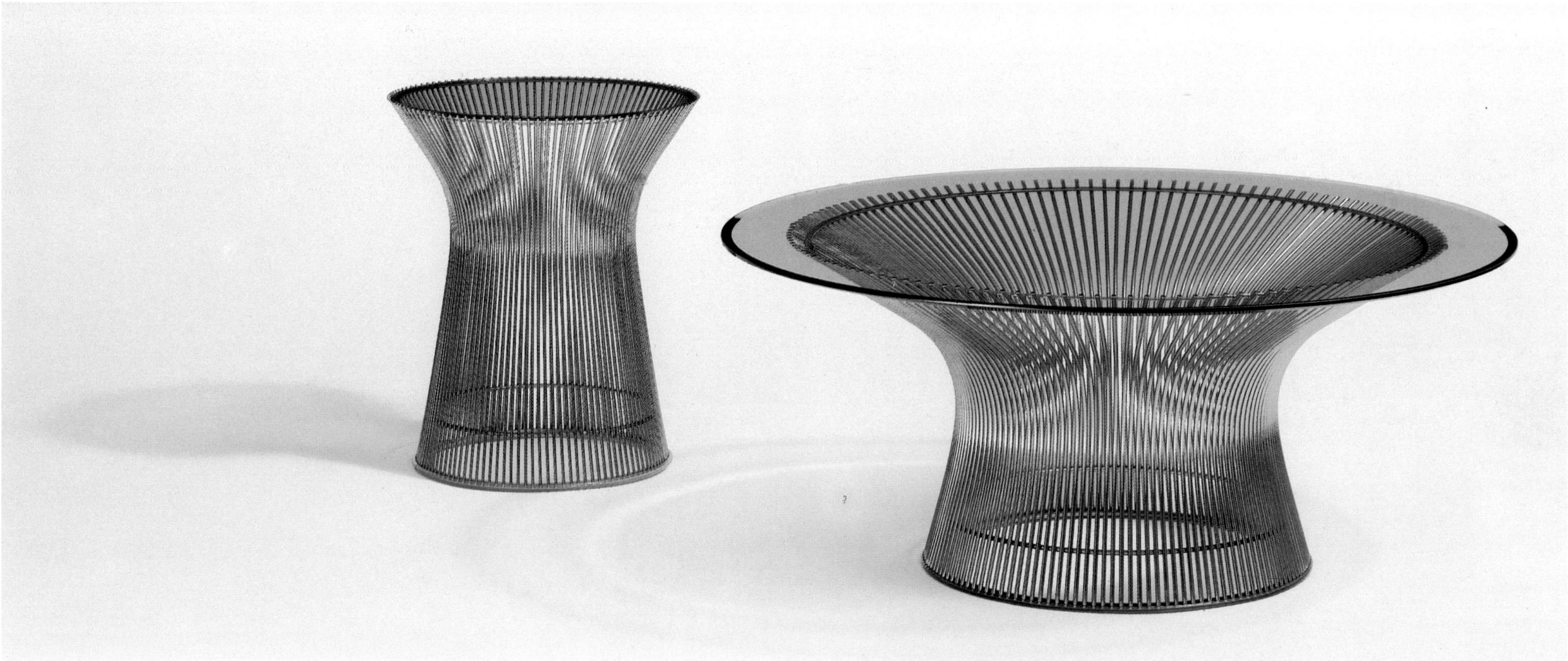

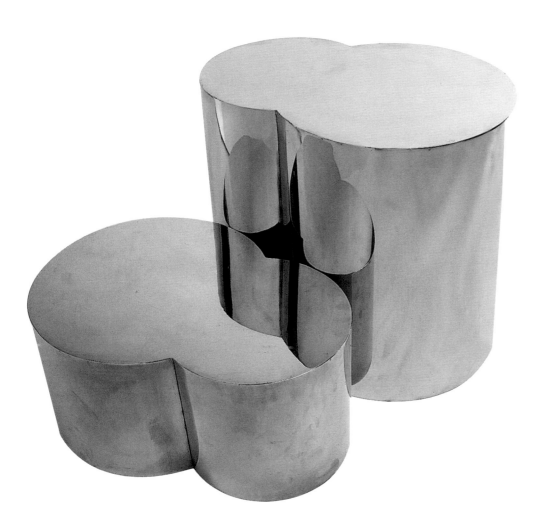

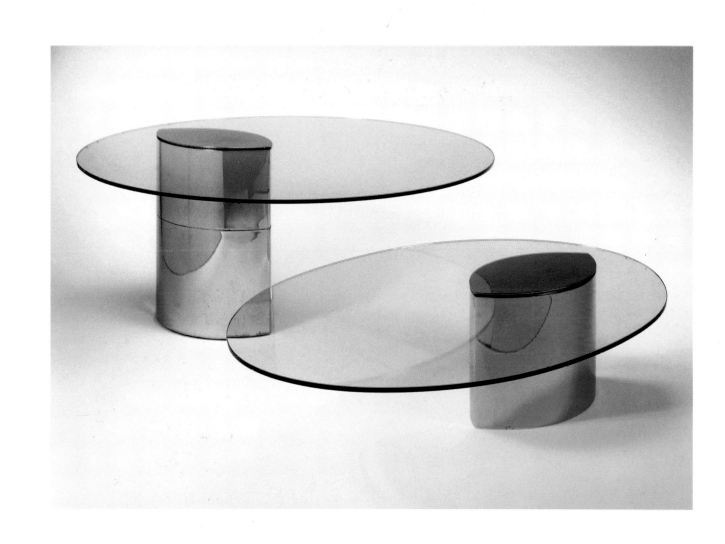

Vico Magistretti
Caori, circa 1962
In situ with furniture from the
Bastano range by Tobia Scarpa.

148

95. Superstudio
Quaderna, 1969

Luigi Colani
Pool living pad, 1970-1971
The desire for the informal
seating area this time
integrates the coffee table into
the plane of the pad

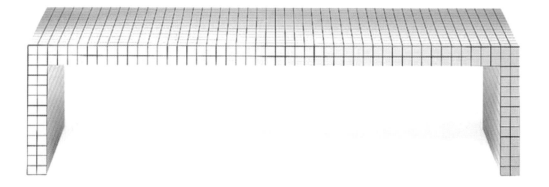

96. Shiro Kuramata,
low table, 1976

97. Shiro Kuramata
Luminous table, 1969

Allen Jones
table, 1969
From a series of three
fetishistic female figures cast
in an edition of six. The group
consisted of a coat stand, chair
and the table, pictured here.
This table has been referred to
as erotic, misogynistic and
sadistic.

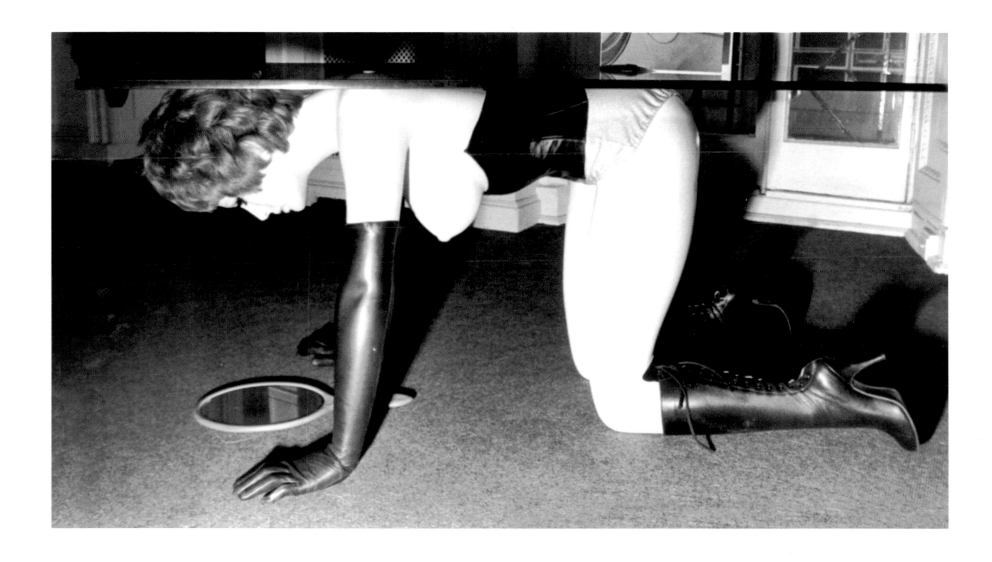

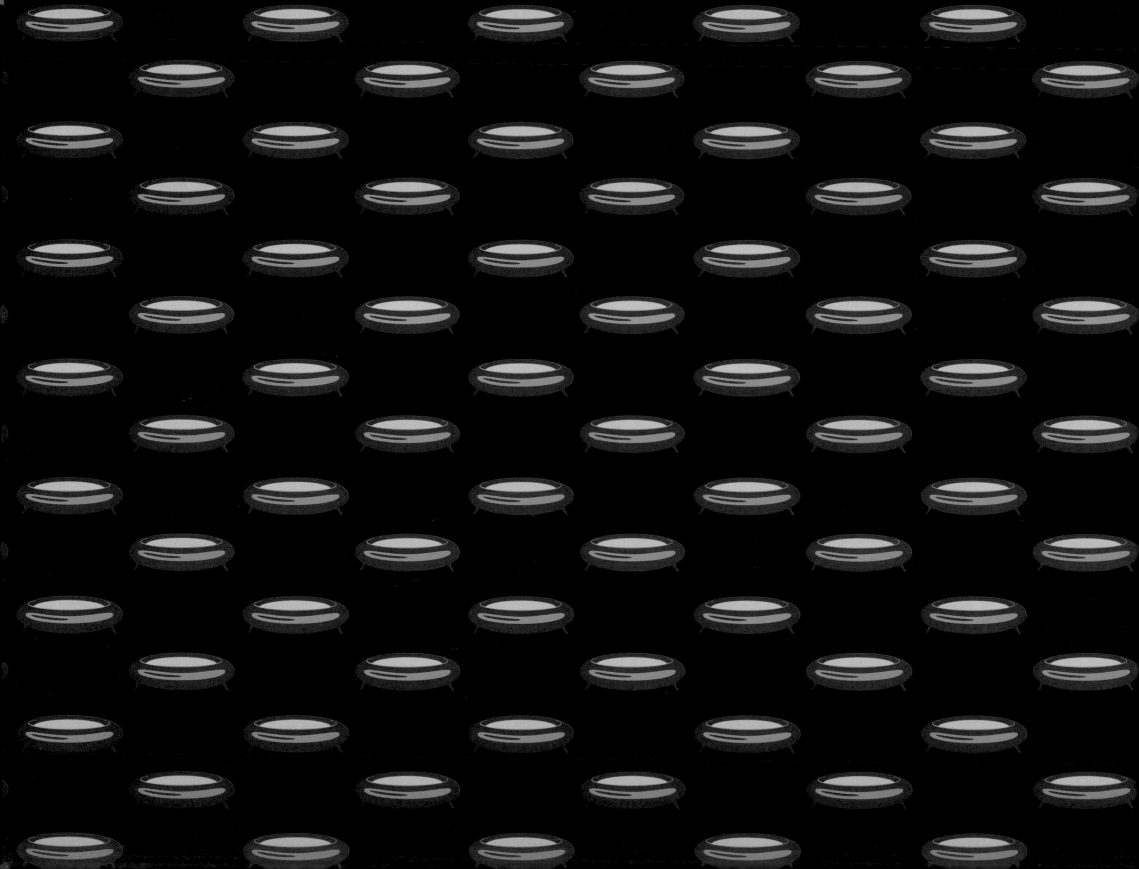

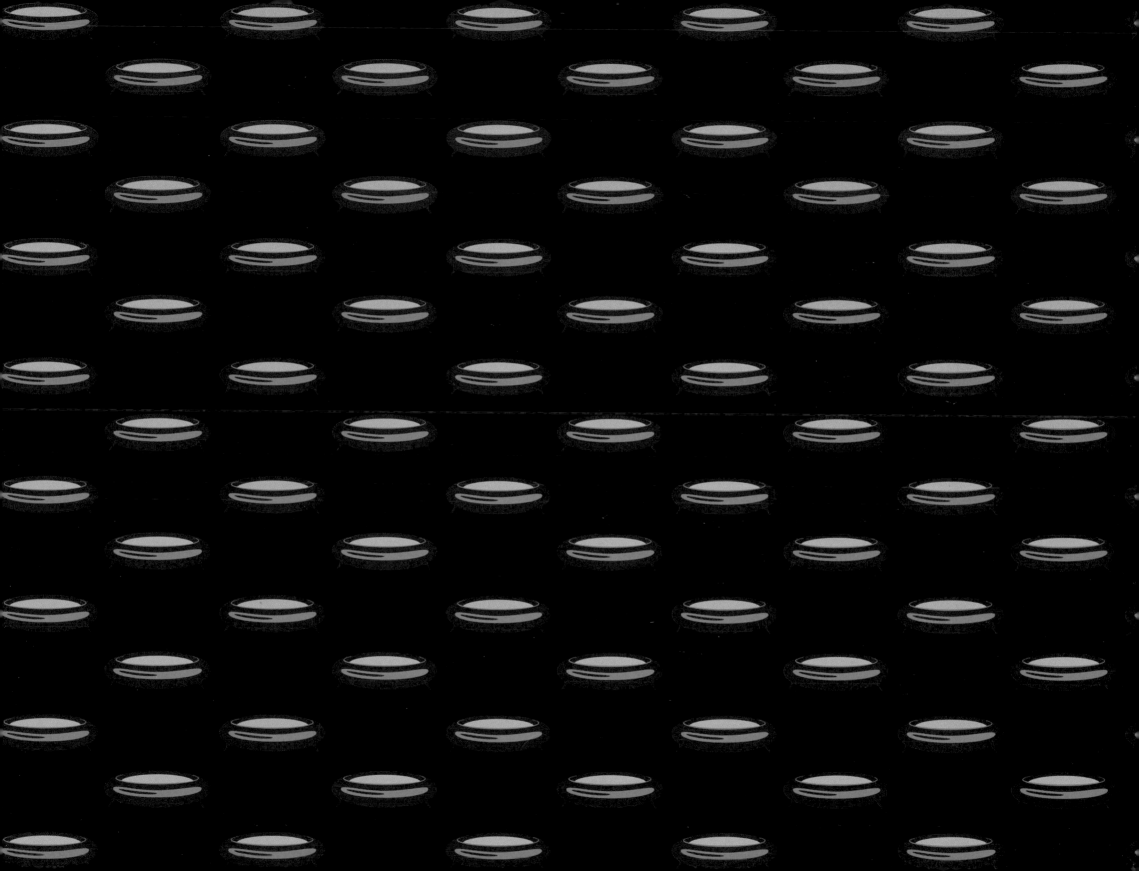

six

from memphis to mutant materials

Designers in the late 1970s and early 80s were confronted with a new market-based economy, the thirst of consumerism, and an increase in cultural commentary. Postmodernism had arrived. Products for the home were no longer designed as signifiers of modernism, industrialism, democracy or utopianism.

In his Learning from Milan Andea Branzi argued that designers must create their own markets for their products. Out of the radical design movements of the 1960s came Alessandro Mendini and Ettore Sottsass, Studio Alchemia and Memphis, their new ideas based on manifestos of 're-design' and 'banal design'. These designers gave birth to objects that existed in their own design universe, made with love and meant to last. They also spawned a garish stylistic period when laminates, colour and the pairing of precious and semi-precious metals were all key players in the application of exaggerated detailing and the decoration of objects, while at the same time paying homage to earlier styles, from Chippendale to Art Deco.

But who outside of the Domus-reading minority could fathom such rhetoric and actually live with it? For the coffee table, low on the totem pole of trend signifiers purchased by the design cognoscenti (as opposed to the chair), it was a dark time. None of the following examples of this period are ever remembered by curators forming a survey of twentieth century design.

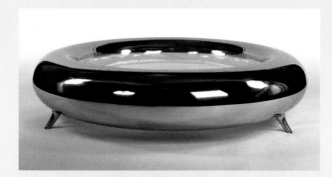

Mendini's Ondoso coffee table of 1980, for Alchimia, epitomised
the Italian group's decorative rebellion against industrial
constraints and the requirements of the marketplace. Its
laminated Formica-style surface was the Alchimia/Memphis
calling card, while its form gave a nod to 1950s style, with its
biomorphic shape and slim stiletto legs harking back to the
works of Carlo Mollino. Yet it certainly wouldn't have fit in
comfortably with the 'democracy' of the 50s interior. The Park
Lane table, by Sottsass for Memphis, was, again, a spectacular
work of art, taking on board the new ideas in its sculptural
base of marble and fibreglass.

101. Alessandro Mendini
Ondoso, 1980
This table is by the predecessors
of the Memphis group, Studio
Alchimia, and forms part of a set
of designs by Mendini known as
the Bauhaus I Collection. The
amoebic shaped surface and legs
refered to 1950s style.

102. Ettore Sottsass
Park Lane, 1983
This epitomises the Memphis
groups' mixing of materials,
here with the use of fibreglass
and marble.

Interior of a Miami home, 2001
In the foreground, Yves Klein, table bleue, 1961,
which is produced anually in a limited series.

Other postmodern designers including Michael Graves, Robert Venturi and Charles Jencks argued for a return to symbolism in architecture and design. Venturi's furniture, for Knoll in the 1980s, was, perhaps, a successful example of historicism made simple for the marketplace, blending "look at me" colour and showmanship with a form that was easily integrated into a domestic interior. Venturi blanketed his coffee tables from this series with 'supergraphics' famously learnt from his studies of Las Vegas signage—a semiotic way of blending historicism onto a surface rather than in its form.

During the same period as the rise of postmodernism, a similar move back to the past was seen in the continued growth of the Craft Revival. In England, John Makepeace re-established the artisan traditions of the Arts and Crafts Movement of the nineteenth century. In New York, weekenders continued to make the journey across the Delaware River to walk in the woods with George Nakashima, whose organic coffee table tops cut from cross-sections of trees with exquisite craftsmanship grew more baroque with the passing years. Meanwhile, deep-pocketed 'crafties' throughout America succumbed to the marketing of Wendell Castle, whose skills as a carpenter and sculptor and the sinuous forms first seen in his Pop plastic designs were allowed to flower, unchecked, into monstrous vines, endowed with such headshaking titles as No Excuses. And thus the 1980s also witnessed the lamentable genre dubbed "art furniture", still alive today and epitomised by the annual SOFA fairs of New York and Chicago, where earnest couples wearing elaborate jewellery seek out unique coffee tables for their living spaces, each example constructed with superb craftsmanship, expensive materials, and an appalling lack of good taste.

103. Ali Tayar
NEA Table 1, 1995
Upon discovering a particleboard
skid on the sidewalk in New York's
Meatpacking District, Ali Tayar
carried it home and incorporated it
into the table.

But what are the general public buying for their living rooms? There is little doubt that the term "coffee table" was integrated into everyday vocabulary with increasing frequency as the decades passed. Literally thousands of TV shows were filmed in the 1980s from the perspective of the viewer looking into the living room at the actors sitting on couches behind coffee tables, apparently mirroring the activities of the viewer. An unending variety of anonymous coffee tables had feet put on them, drinks spilled across them and bowls of popcorn placed in front of Dad, kids and Mom. But for the vast populace, the coffee table was a generic rectangle, a piece that required less thought when purchased than the chairs, sofas and dining room suite. For the most part, it was a tasteful 'country number', or a glass and steel platform faintly echoing, again, the International Style.

But the lessons taught by the Postmodernists did have an impact on the next generation of designers. The keyword that emerged from all this was recycling. Whether it was earlier design movements or the everyday objects of the interior and vernacular landscapes, recycling as a cultural term was the predominant theme of design collectives, including Droog Design in the Netherlands and Boym Studio in New York. Recycling as an environmental term, and the rise of the Greens had an impact on designers such as Ron Arad, Danny Lane, Tom Dixon and JAM. Indeed, JAM were dubbed "the sultans of scrap", as they scavenged aeronautic and household refuse sites in search of objects discarded by the wasteful, and which could then be used in their designs. The Nea Table 1, 1992, by Ali Tayar, used a particleboard skid reclaimed near the designer's home in New York's Meatpacking District placed on bespoke aluminium feet. Tayar had mirrored the recycling concept applied in the film *Blow Up*, 1967, where two painted wine racks were used to support a glass top and thus create a coffee table. Tayar's second version, Nea Table 2, was exhibited in 1995 at the Museum of Modern Art's *Mutant Materials* exhibition, a platform that showed the 'new wave' of designers utilising

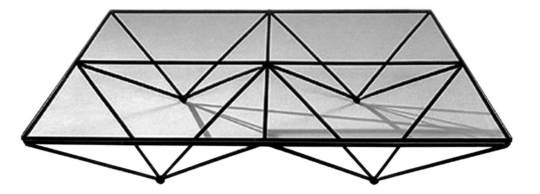

164

the ever increasing array of resources available to them.

As we moved further into the 1990s and nearer to the Millennium the strength of the economy spawned an increase in retailers' marketing a sleek, homogenous 'shelter' concept, with home improvements, style and interior design being showcased heavily throughout the media. New TV shows such as *Frasier* and *Sex in the City* popularised what it was like to live a sophisticated, urban life in the late twentieth century and provided a platform for advertising what were the must-have design classics—the obligatory Eames Lounge Chair and Ottoman, perhaps a curvy, bright-coloured Panton S chair, or the looming presence of Castiglione's Arco floor lamp. The tastefully 'Modern' coffee table on the set was now the place to display books on art, photography and design along with magazines like *Elle Decor* and *Wallpaper*—which complete the circle of subliminal design propaganda by inviting us to see how we should be living. If there is room in the dictionary for the terms coffee table and coffee table book, should we now be asking, is there the place to add a definition for "coffee table magazine"? Also interesting here is the general recycling of earlier decades' greatest hits as the anchors for these newly sophisticated interiors. While the individuality of the coffee table was frequently de-emphasised on both TV sets and fashion shoots, it did mean newfound

Wallpaper* Launch Issue
September/October 1996
Under the editorial direction of
Tyler Brûlé Wallpaper* became
a global style magazine helping
to create a 'wallpaper
generation' of design
aficionados.

popularity amongst consumers for such design classics as the Barcelona and IN-50
tables, which were either reissued or marketed with renewed vigour.
After Philippe Starck defined the trend of the superstar designer in the 1980s, the 90s
also witnessed the phenomenon of designers becoming the new "Heroes of Style", and
being placed now, unsurprisingly, alongside actors and musicians as cultural icons. To
be a designer or a design groupie was super cool, and to recognise good design was a
mark of style, flair and being in the know. In England, 'designer' bands opened clubs,
bars and restaurants while in such hip outposts as Reykjavik the talents of England's
hottest designers were put to use. Starck joined forces with Ian Shrager and opened
hotels across Europe and America, using furniture as stage props for the nightly
bacchanals of the wealthy young Internet generation. And for every lobby bar grouping of
Starck seating or Pesce props, there had to be the requisite low coffee table for the
ashtrays and *Cosmopolitan*s.

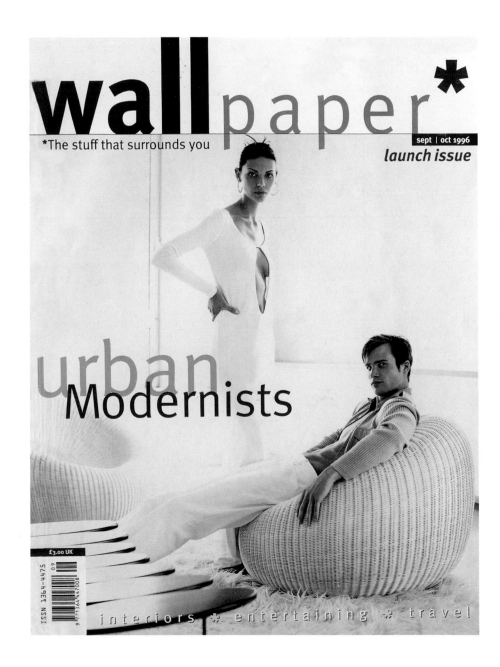

105. Dunne & Raby
Compass Table, 2001
from the Placebo collection
The 25 compasses set into the
table twitch and spin when
devices with electro-magnetic
and information 'hanging in the
air', such as lap tops and
mobile phones, come into the
table's proximity.

166

Today, designers are recognised and lauded, as media figures and chameleons; while chairs are still the icons of style that ensure their role in the pantheon of design, designers are more obsessed than ever with creating a multitude of objects—from glassware to office supplies, from dog houses to vibrators—which, in turn, provide more copy for the ever-growing stack of new shelter magazines. An essential chapter in the superstar designer's dossier is the aforementioned bar or restaurant, as seen in recent projects by Marc Newson, Marcel Wanders and Micheal Young. The coffee table too has become chameleon-like, made to fit its environment, whether domestic or public, and symbolic of the individual 'style' practiced by the superstar designer, be it the Orgone shapes of Newson, or its low-cost derivatives in the designs of Karim Rashid. If anything, every memorable coffee table of the 1990s and early twenty-first century is wildly

disparate, the result of so much available technology, so many historical precedents, so broad a spectrum of cultural referencing, and, of course, the pressure on each designer to create a unique branding.

New environmental concerns are being addressed too. Noise, environmental pollution and electromagnetic stress, for example—the direct results of the way in which we live in the early twenty-first century—have prompted some designers to reflect on the impact of these through their work. The electromagnetic fields that surround us have been poignantly illustrated by Dunne and Raby's Compass Table, where compasses set into a table's top spin in panic when picking up electromagnetic waves generated by the mobile phones, televisions and other electronic goods we have come to rely on.

And new domestic concerns have also been addressed. The lack of space in

106. Gae Aulenti
coffee table, 1980

107. Rei Kawakubo
pair of Grey Triangler tables, 1985

108. Tomoko Azumi
Table=Chest, 1999
This piece of flexible furniture
moves from table to chest and
vice versa—a cross between
transformer and choreography.

modern apartments has prompted the design of "dual furniture", offering the user a multi-purpose object with its place in the home being thus justified. With this in mind, there have been some truly new takes on the coffee table; in the same way that tables in the 1950s were produced with low tiers or side shelves for the storage of books and magazines, we have more recently seen some clever flexible furniture. The Azumis have created ingenious designs, such as Table=Chest, which morphs in a single, beautifully choreographed movement from a chest of drawers to a coffee table. Four Forty, by Michael Solis, cleverly overcomes one of the nagging problems for the music-lover living with stacks of CDs cluttering up the floor by opening to reveal a secret chamber for disc storage. In a parody of the multi-tasking done by short-attention span professionals at health clubs, Spaniard Hector Serrano's coffee table From Infinity and Beyond presents its owner with the opportunity to exercise while partaking of that inherently modern-day pastime, watching tv, as what on first sight is a coffee table becomes a trampoline.

109. Hector Serrano and Lola Llorca
From Infinity to Beyond, 2001
From the "Manolo is Gonna Have
Fun" collection. The table as an
object of fun—when it is not
required to be a coffee table it can
be used as a trampoline.

And there is the unending availability of new technologies and processes. Wanders' Lace Table combines computer generated technology with a nod to the handicraft, his design beautifully creating the illusion of a lace tablecloth thrown over an invisible cube, frozen for eternity. Computer rendering has provided new methods for conceptualising design, becoming an area of investigation in its own right for the designer to explore. In an age when anything seems possible the only boundary is the designer's own imagination.

Will the living room change its face once again and the coffee table be replaced by a new breed of object, or will the coffee table of the future have to communicate and offer multiple uses in a more radical way? Perhaps the coffee table will become more nomadic, like its owner, wandering from room to room as the boundaries of each room blur and technology follows people around. These and other similar questions are posed and responded to by today's designers. The remote controlled table FreeWheelin' Franklin from Jerzy Seymour with its Big Foot tyres and height-adjustable tray top offers us that perfectly delivered cup of coffee wherever we want it—the next best thing to a robot so far? Perhaps the domestic landscape of the early twenty-first century, as dreamed up by designers like Nick Crosbie and the Bouroullec brothers will indeed be different. Their pioneering ideas—concept interiors described to us through computer models—continue to creatively push the dialogue between user and object, expanding into fantasy 'innerscapes' for the twenty-first century.

111. Barber Osgerby
Loop tables, 1997
the Loop's offset leg creates an
illusion of the table floating

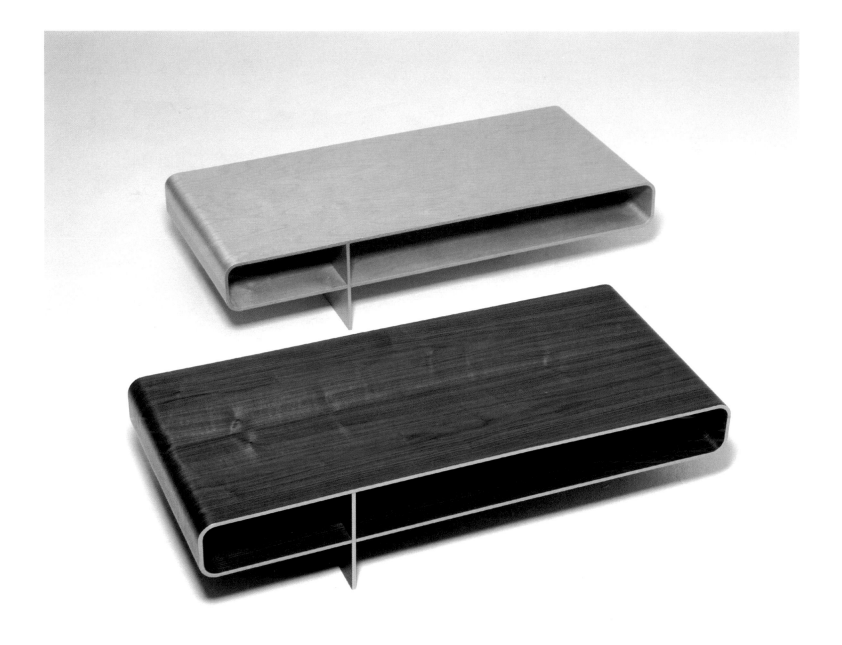

112. El Ultimo Grito
Mind the Gap, 1998
The table's top and form
dictates the shape of the rubber
with the rubber falling through
the gap we have been warned
of! The result is a pocket for
books and magazines.

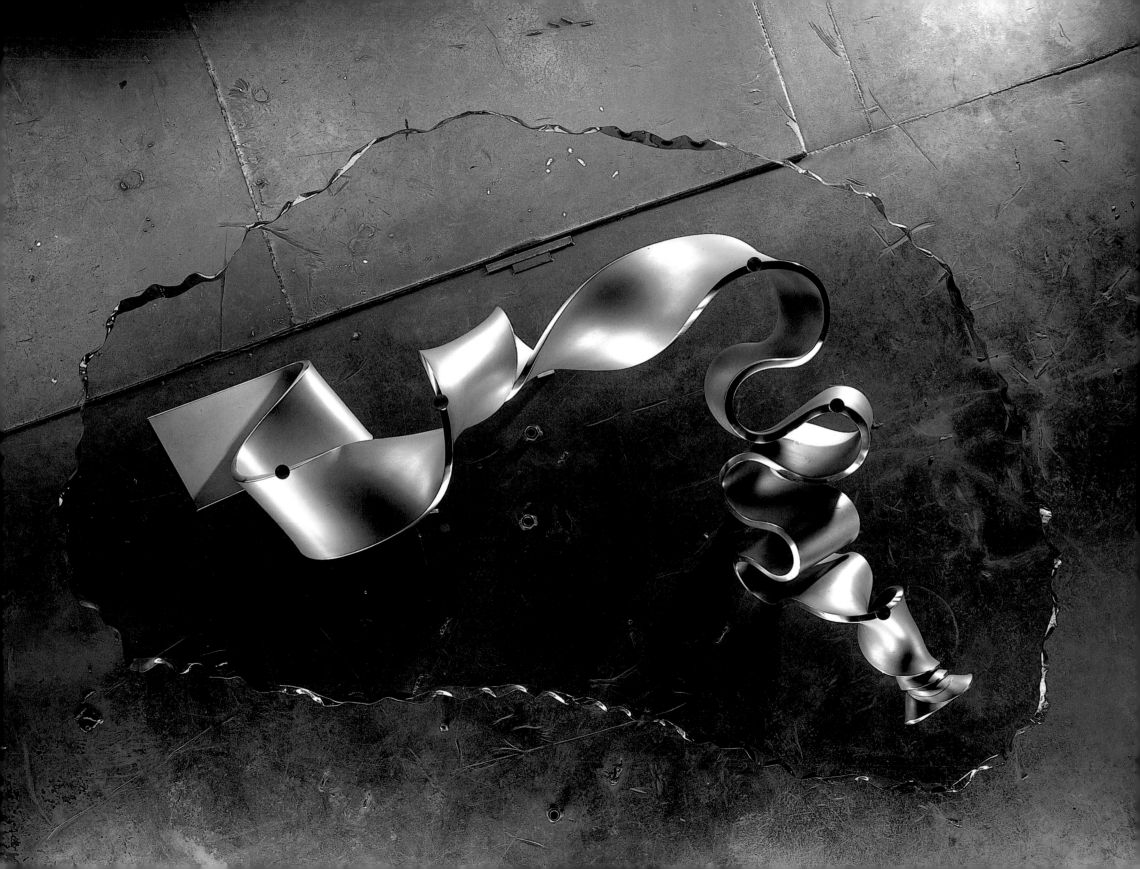

113. Danny Lane
Tagliatelle, 1997
Lane combines the fragile with
the tough. The steel in his
sculptural work is twisted and
formed intro seemingly
impossible poses.

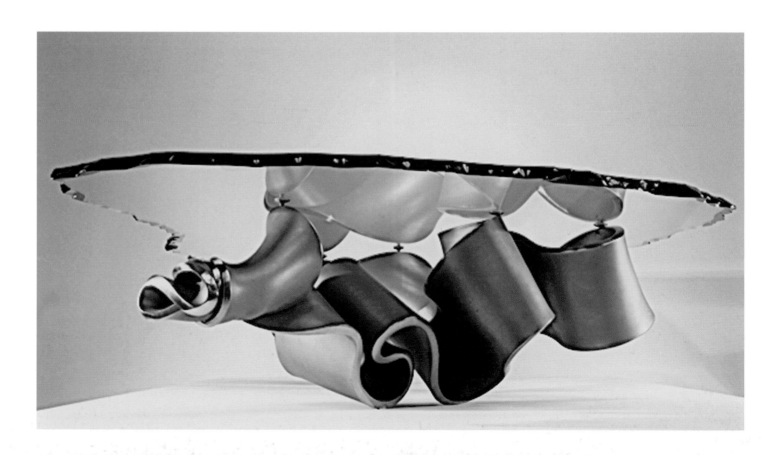

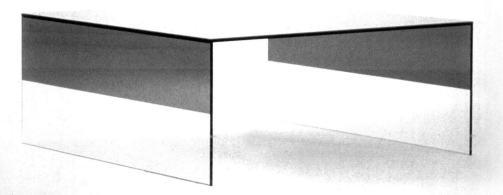

115. Michael Young
Wagon, 2000

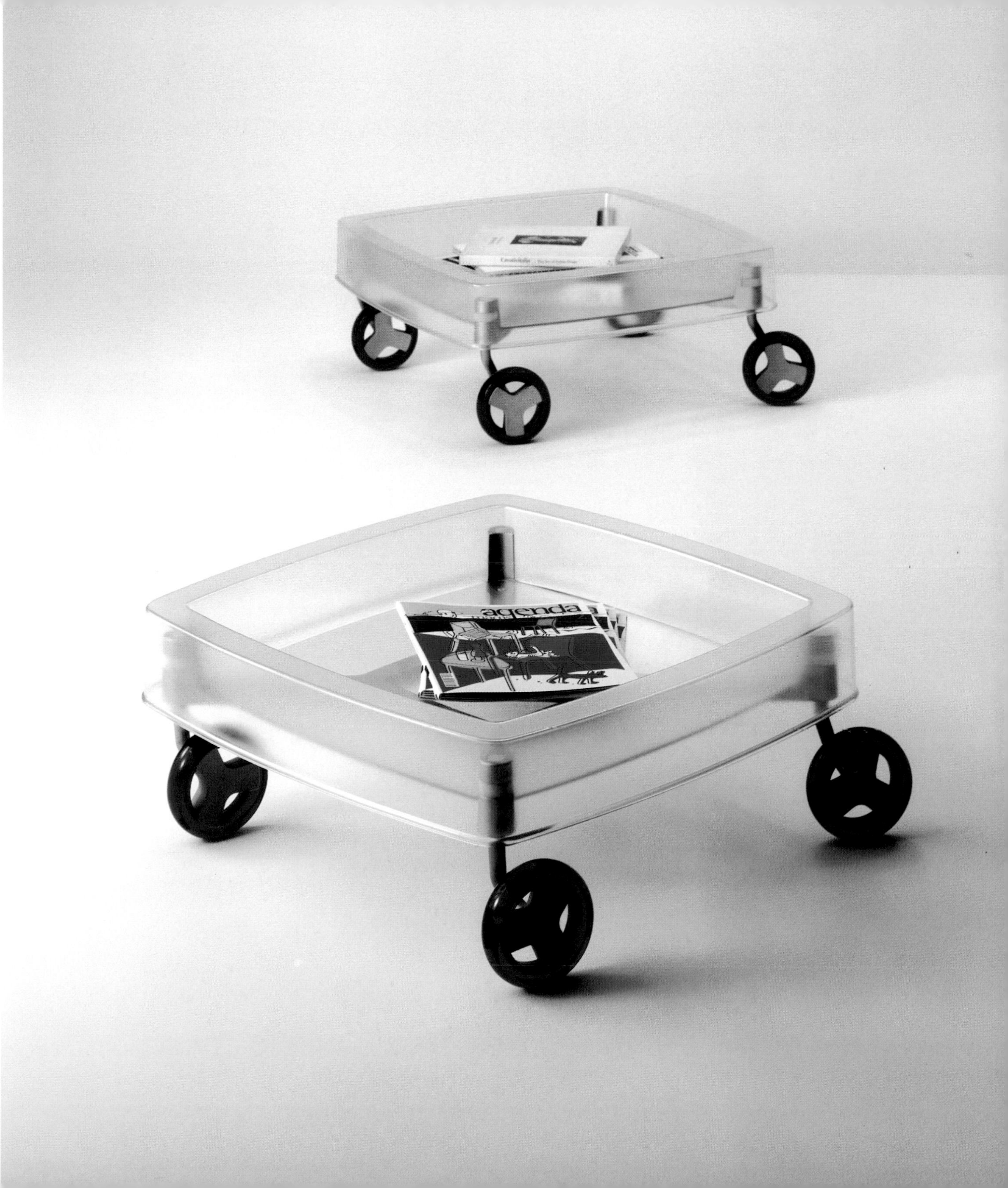

116. Lorenzo Damiani
Tavolante table and lamp, 1999
Tavolante's lamp can be lowered
into the table to create an
ambient light or raised above it
as a chandelier.

117. Ron Arad
B.O.O.P. (Blown Out Of Proportion), 1998
An 'inflated' aliminium table, produced
by cavity forming without the use of
moulds—superplastic aluminium sheet is
heated and then inflated through large
steel stencils.

118. Shin + Tomoko Azumi
hm30 low table, 2001
The hm range consists of
asymmetric seating units with
sofas that can be used alone, or
combined with a corner ottoman
to create larger flexible seating
arrangements. The low coffee
tables, with etched glass,
complete the scene.

119. Michael Young
MY07 Magazine Table, 1995
From Young's first collection of
22 objects, the designer here
draws attention to the
significance of the magazine.
An answer to the question as to
whether or not there should be a
magazine table as well as a
coffee table.

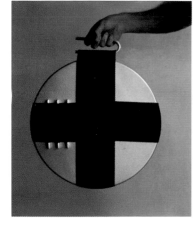
Inflatable Table—flat packed

122. The Campana Brothers
Inflatable Table, 2001

184

123. Marcel Wanders
Lace Table, 1997

124. The Campana Brothers
cardboard table, 2001
Taking banal materials such as
bubble wrap (bubble wrap
chair), cardboard (cardboard
chair and table) and garden-
hose (garden-hose chair), the
Brothers magically turn these
materials into some of the
finest and most unique designs
of the day.

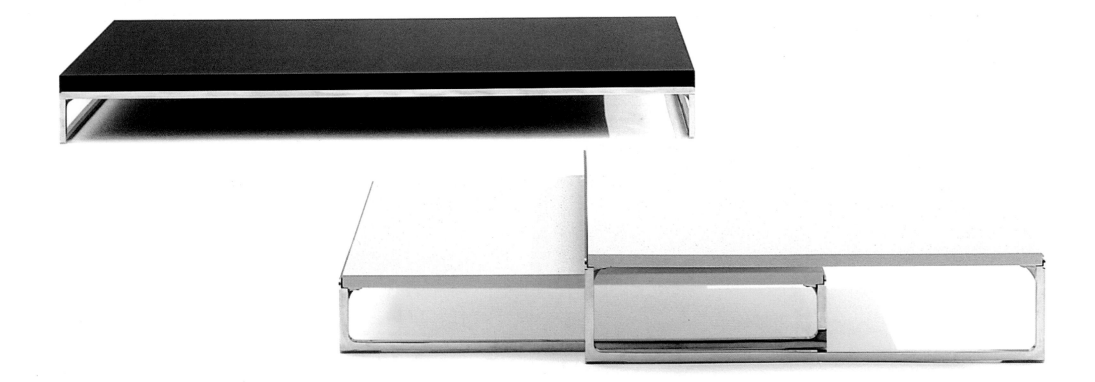

126. Michael Sodeau
Satellite Table, 1997

127. Marcel Wanders
Knotted Table, 2001
In a surprising marriage of
handcraft and industrial
technology—Macramé meets
high-tech.

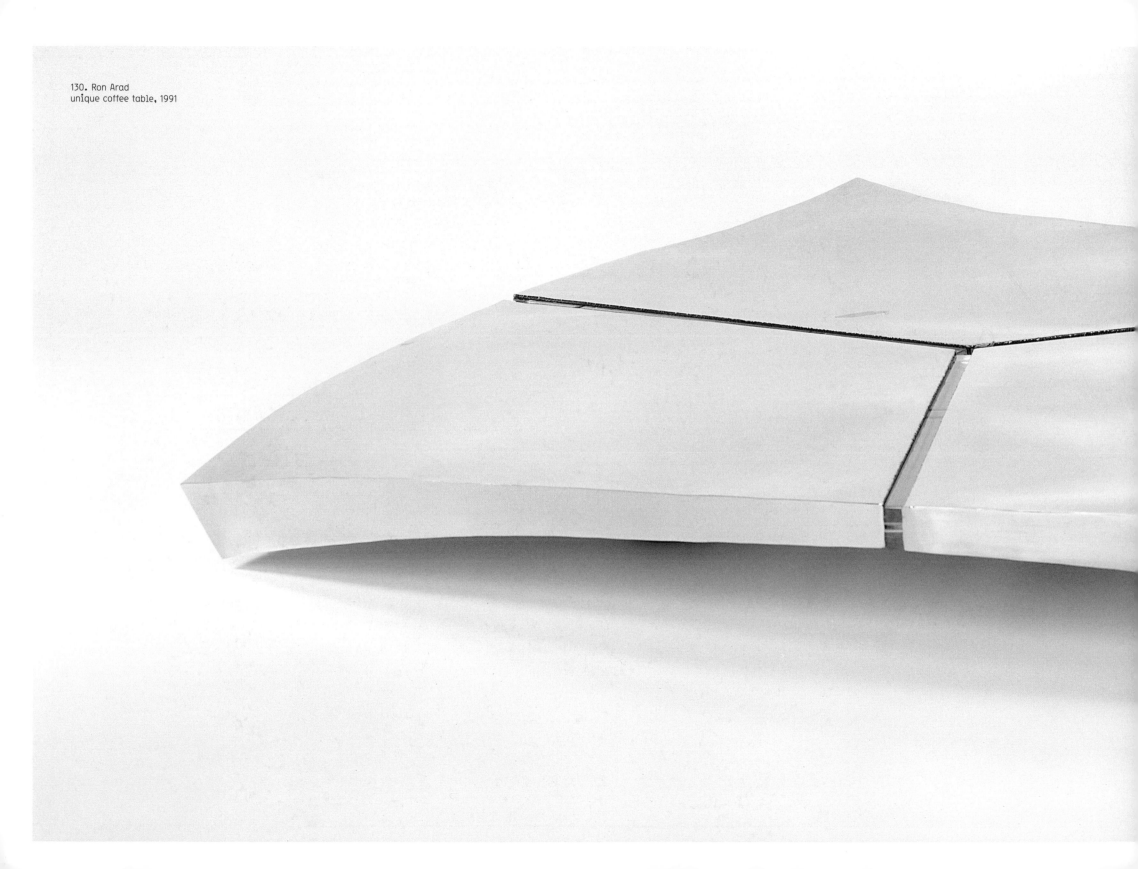

130. Ron Arad
unique coffee table, 1991

131. Joan Gasper
Sydney, 2000
The top surface of Sydney slides along the lower shelf
revealing and hiding objects.

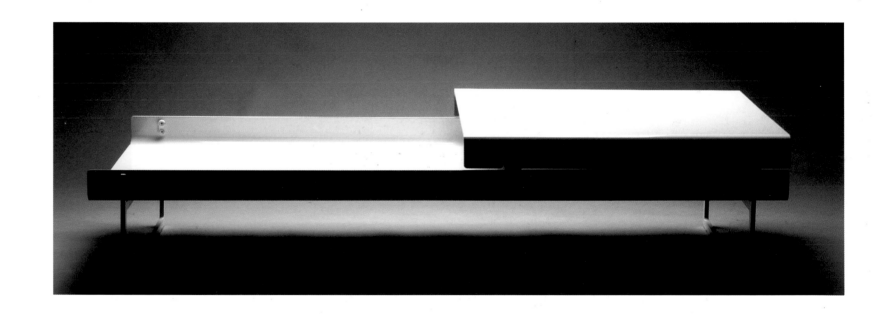

133. Martin Szekely
coffee table M.G.D., 2002

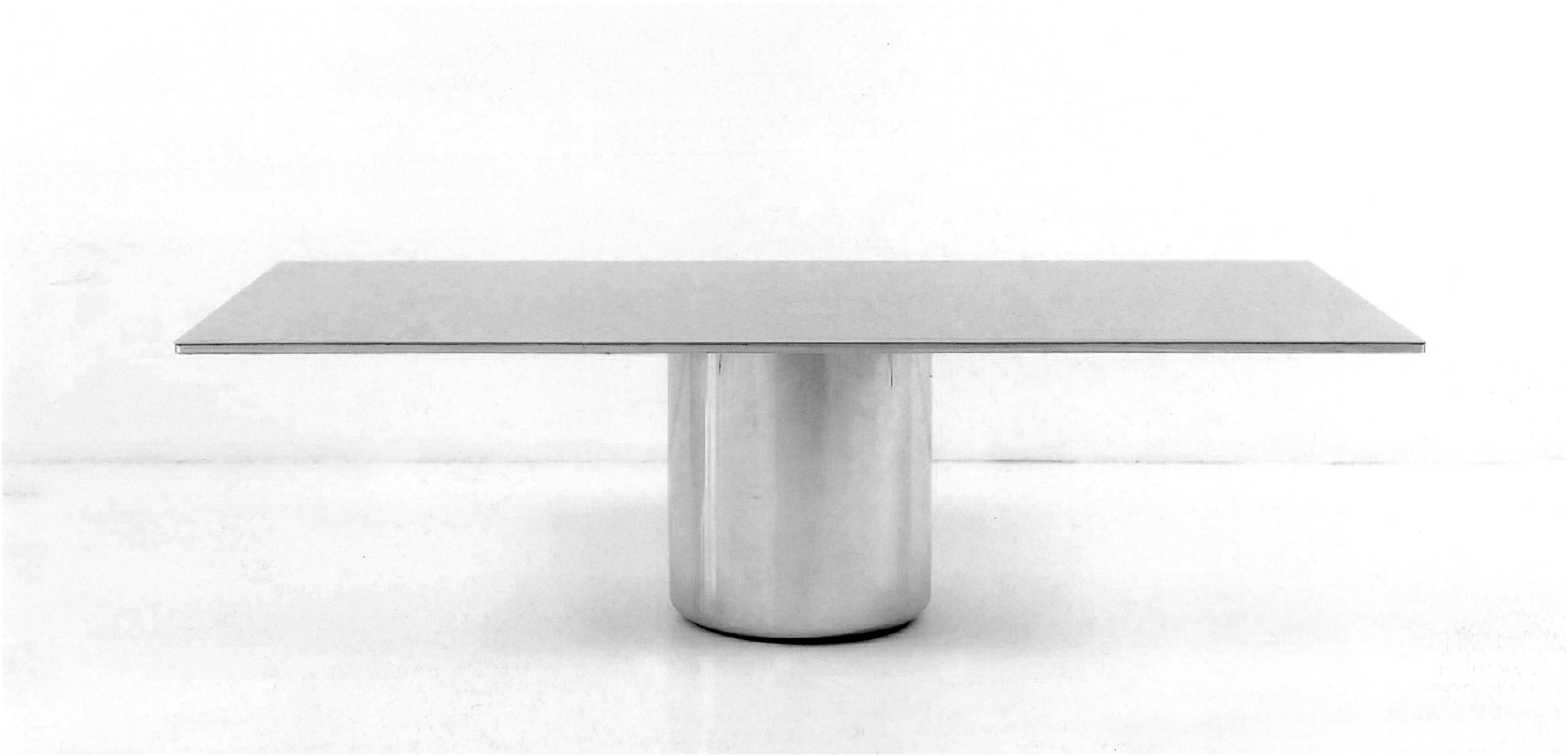

CHAPTER 1

1. Marcel Wanders
Flower Table, 2001
produced by Moooi
luan wood with burnt-in flower
illustration
30 x 120 cm
courtesy of the designer

Jean Royère
project for the salon à la maison de
France à Rio de Janeiro,
circa 1950
courtesy of Musée des Arts décoratifs,
Paris

2. JAM
Flatscreen Coffee Table, 1999
produced by JAM with Sony
Wega screen, MDF base and wheels
25 x 46 x 72 cm
courtesy of the designers

Herman Miller Archive, 1948
courtesy of Herman Miller archive

3. Boym Studio
Coffee Table Book Table, 1992
from the Searstyle Collection
plywood, books ("The Presidents")
courtesy of the designers
© Constantin Boym

Jacques-Emile Ruhlmann
Boudoir-library, 1918

Herman Miller Catalogue, 1940
courtesy of Herman Miller
© Hedrich-Blessing Studio

Ikea
Lack, 2001
courtesy of Ikea

4. Isamu Noguchi
IN-52, 1949
manufactured by Herman Miller
1949-1950
birch and aluminum
87.6 x 38.5 x 124.5 cm
courtesy of Phillips,
de Pury & Luxembourg

CHAPTER 2

5. Eileen Gray
Bilboquet table, circa 1915
lacquered wood with
silvered details on legs
courtesy of Philippe Garner

Jacques Doucet's salon
L'Illustration, May 1930
courtesy of Phi
lipe Garner

6. Jacques-Emile Ruhlmann
basse bouille, 1918-1919
ébène de macassar
courtesy of Musée des Arts décoratifs,
Paris

Jacques-Emile Ruhlmann
apartment for the dress designer
Fernarde Cabanel

Jacques-Emile Ruhlmann
Chambre de jeune fils, 1920-22
courtesy of Philippe Garner

7. Jacques-Emile Ruhlmann
Colonette Table, circa 1920-1922
ébène de macassar and ivory
42.2 x 80.3 cm
courtesy of Phillips,
de Pury & Luxembourg

Charlotte Perriand
Le Bars sous le Toit, 1927

Francis Jourdain
Project de Studio, circa 1925-30
courtesy of Musée des Arts décoratifs,
Paris

8. Jean-Michel Frank
Table basse, circa 1930
veneered panels of shagreen
49 x 40.5 x 109 cm
© Christie's Images Ltd, 2003

Armand Rateau, L' Appartment de
Jeanne Lanvin, 1920-22

9. Armand Rateau
table basse for L'Appartement
de Jeanne Lanvin, model no. 1209,
1920-1922
patinated bronze
courtesy of Musée des Arts décoratifs,
Paris

10. Ludwig Mies van der Rohe
Barcelona coffee table
manufactured by Knoll International
1948-present day
stainless steel, glass
43.3 x 101.6 x 101.6 cm
courtesy of Knoll, Inc

11. Ludwig Mies van der Rohe
Tugendhat coffee table
manufactured by Knoll International
1964-present day
courtesy of Knoll Inc

12. Ludwig Mies van der Rohe
Table for the Barcelona Pavilion,
Berlin 1928
Chrome-plated metal, glass
Neue Galerie, New York
©2003 Neue Galerie
photograph by David Schiegel

Ludwig Mies van der Rohe
Seagram Building lobby, New York 1958
The Seagram Collection of Photographs
Courtesy of Phillips,
de Pury & Luxembourg
Photograph by Erza Stoller

CHAPTER 3

13. Donald Deskey
cocktail table, 1927-1931
manufactured by Deskey-Vollmer, Inc,
New York
steel, Vitrolite glass
37.9 x 61 cm
courtesy of Phillips,
de Pury & Luxembourg

Paul Frankl
modern living room
from an exhibition at
Abraham & Strauss, Brooklyn

14. Gilbert Rohde
Rotorette, 1929
black lacquered wood, leatherette,
metal and Vitrolite glass
46.3 x 63.8 cm
collection of Mr and Mrs Lee M Rohde,
Chappaqua, NY
photograph by Richard Goodbody

Russel Wright
Living Room, East 40th Street, New
York, circa 1937
courtesy Russel L Wright
Department of Special Collections,
Syracuse University Library

Walter Dorwin Teague
Decorative Art 1939 Yearbook
© Eileen Tweedy
courtesy of Thames and Hudson

15. Russel Wright
revolving coffee table, circa 1934
black plastic laminate, plywood and
chromium-plated tubular steel
43.2 cm high
collection of William Straus, New York
photograph by Richard Goodbody

16. Frederick Kiesler
table with lamp from the
Mergentine interior, 1935
chromium-plated tubular steel
and glass
45.7 x 114.3 cm
private collection, New York
photograph by Richard Goodbody

Frederick Kiesler
Drawing for Furniture, 1935
Frederick Kiesler Centre, Vienna
courtesy of the Austrian Frederick and
Lillian Kiesler Private Foundation

Herman Miller Archive, 1940
courtesy of Herman Miller

17. unknown American designer
low table, circa 1937
plate glass
41.3 x 91.4 cm
courtesy of The Metropolitan Museum of
Art, New York, gift of Mr and Mrs Victor
Gaines, (1976, 417ab)
© 2000 The Metropolitan Museum of Art

18. Gilbert Rohde
coffee table model no. 3944, 1939-1940
manufactured by Herman Miller,
Zeeland, MI
Lucite
39.5 x 56 x 112 cm
courtesy of Wright
Brian Franczyk Photography

Marcel Breuer and Walter Gropius
The Frank House
Pittsburgh, Pennsylvania, 1939
Photograph by Ezra Stoller

Marcel Breuer
living room at Heals, London,
April 1936
© The Board of the Trustees of the
Victoria and Albert Museum
courtesy of Heals Archive and V&A
Picture Library

Edward Durrell Stone
the Goodyear House, Old Westbury, Long
Island, 1939

19. Wolfgang Hoffmann
coffee tables, model no. 803, 1934
manufactured by Howell Company,
St. Charles, IL, circa 1934-1942
chromium-plated steel and glass
43 x 66 cm
43 x 81.5 cm
courtesy of Phillips,
de Pury & Luxembourg

20. Warren McArthur
coffee table, circa 1930s
manufactured by Warren McArthur
Corporation, Rome, NY
aluminum, wood and rubber
44.5 x 89 x 44 x 90 cm
courtesy of Wright
Brian Franczyk Photography

21. Denham MacLaren
coffee table, 1936
black lacquered wood and glass
private collection, London

22. Denham MacLaren
sculpture/coffee table, 1936
white-lacquered wood and glass
103.5 x 22 cm
courtesy of Phillips,
de Pury & Luxembourg

Denham MacLaren
two tables for Duncan Miller,
London, 1936

23. Frederick Kiesler
nesting coffee table, 1935-1938
cast aluminum
courtesy of the Austrian Frederick and
Lillian Kiesler Private Foundation

24. Frederick Kiesler
nesting coffee table, 1935-1938
unique custom produced
cast aluminium
37.5 x 99 cm
private collection, New York
photograph by Richard Goodbody

25. Gilbert Rohde
coffee table model no. 4188, 1940
manufactured by Herman Miller,
Zeeland, MI
paldao walnut, acacia burl and leather
42 x 114.4 x 114.4 cm
private collection, New York
photograph by Richard Goodbody

Gilbert Rohde
Herman Miller advertisement, Fall 1940
courtesy of Herman Miller

26. Eileen Gray
Free-Form Table from Tempe à Pailla,
circa 1935
textured wood and chromed metal
45.5 x 99 x 51.5 cm
courtesy of Phillips,
de Pury & Luxembourg

27. Paul Dupré-Lafon
table basse, circa 1930s
marble and iron
courtesy of L'Arc en Seine Gallery,
Paris

28. T H Robsjohn-Gibbings
low table from the Casa Encantada,
Bel Air, CA, circa 1937
manufactured by Peterson Studios,
Los Angeles
oak and glass
50.8 x 108 x 47 cm
courtesy of Phillips,
de Pury & Luxembourg

29. Maison Jansen
table basse, circa 1940
painted gilt iron and
mirrored glass top
33 x 94 x 60 cm
courtesy of Phillips,
de Pury & Luxembourg

30. Marcel Breuer
low table, circa 1936
manufactured by Isokon
bent and laminated plywood
48 x 69.5 x 68.5 cm
courtesy of Phillips,
de Pury & Luxembourg

Marcel Breuer
cut-out plywood sofa and coffee table,
1939

31. Kaare Klimt
low table, circa 1930s
courtesy of collection of Vance Trimble,
New York
photograph by Richard Goodbody

32. Charlotte Perriand
low table, circa 1939
oak and marble
courtesy of Orange Group, New York
photograph by Richard Goodbody

33. Tommi Parzinger
coffee table, 1939
produced for Rena Rosenthal, New York
carved, pickled wood and
engraved pewter
courtesy of Liz O' Brien, New York

34. Marc du Plantier
table basse, circa 1934
gilt iron and glass
40 x 140 x 62.2 cm
courtesy of Phillips,
de Pury & Luxembourg

CHAPTER 4

35. Isamu Noguchi
IN-50, 1947
manufactured by Herman Miller,
1946-present
ebonised birch and glass
43 x 127 x 91 cm
courtesy of Phillips,
de Pury & Luxembourg

Knoll Advertisement
interiors, August 1942

36. T H Robsjohn-Gibbings
coffee table, 1943
manufactured by the Widdicomb
Furniture Co
walnut with sorrel finish and glass
43.2 x 136.3 x 78.6 cm
courtesy of Phillips,
de Pury & Luxembourg

Frederick Kiesler
Art of This Century Gallery, New York,
1942
Frederick Kiesler Centre, Vienna
courtesy of the Austrian Frederick and
Lillian Kiesler Private Foundation

Lenore Fini
Study of Reclining Female, circa 1950

House Beautiful, 1958
courtesy of Philippe Garner

37. Poul Kjærholm
PK-61, 1956
manufactured by Kold Christensen
1956-1982, Fritz Hansen 1982-present
black slate and chrome-plated steel
32.4 x 82.5 x 82.5 cm
courtesy of Phillips,
de Pury & Luxembourg

Living room in Peter Moro's apartment,
London, circa 1960
Country Life Picture Magazine Archive
courtesy of June Buck and Country Life
Picture Library

38. Isamu Noguchi
IN-50, 1947
manufactured by Herman Miller,
1946-present in occasional batches
birch and pale green glass
43 x 127 x 91 cm
courtesy of Wright
Brian Franczyk Photography

39. Abel Sorensen
coffee table, 1948
manufactured by Knoll 1948-1954
plywood, walnut veneer with exposed
joint detail and birch legs
43.2 x 58.4 x 152.4 cm
courtesy of Phillips,
de Pury & Luxembourg

40. Piero Chiesa
coffee table, circa 1957
manufactured by Fantana Arte
retailed in America by Singer & Sons
illustrated in Roberto Aloi, *Esempi:
Tavoli, Tavolini, Carrelli, Seconda
Series*, Milan 1955

Samuel Marx
period images of the Joseph Block
Residence, 1948
courtesy of Wright

41. Samuel Marx
coffee table, circa 1948
manufactured by Quigley & Co, Chicago
smoked mirrored glass and wood
courtesy of private collection and
Liz O'Brien, New York

42. Samuel Marx
Book Table for the Joseph Block
Residence, 1948
manufactured by Quigley & Co, Chicago
walnut and glass
46 x 114.5 cm
courtesy of Wright
Brian Franczyk Photography

43. Edward Wormley
coffee table from the Janus Collection,
1956
manufactured by Dunbar
walnut, Tiffany glass tiles
43 x 48.5 x 180.5 cm
courtesy of Wright
Brian Franczyk Photography

44. Edward Wormley
coffee table, model no. 5424, 1950
manufactured by Dunbar, Berne, IN
brass, murano glass tiles
41.3 x 114.6 x 43.8 cm
courtesy Phillips,
de Pury & Luxembourg

45. Carlo Mollino
Arabesque Table, circa 1950
manufactured by Apelli & Varesio,
Turin
plywood, maple veneer,
brass and glass
50.2 x 122 x 49.5 cm
courtesy of Fulvio Ferrari

46. Neil Morris
cloud table, circa 1947
manufactured by H Morris & Co Ltd,
Glasgow
Honduran mahogany and Canadian
betula laminate
107 x 115 x 47 cm
courtesy of Phillips,
de Pury & Luxembourg

Paul McCobb
advertising shot of coffee tables,
circa 1955

47. Charles and Ray Eames
prototype three-legged tray table, 1945
manufactured by the Molded Plywood
Division of Evans Products Company,
Venice, CA
plywood and metal
47 x 88.9 x 58.1 cm
courtesy of Phillips,
de Pury & Luxembourg

48. Charles and Ray Eames
OTW (Occasional Table Wood), 1946
manufactured by the Molded Plywood
Division of Evans Products Company,
Venice, CA, 1946-1949
molded plywood with a rare colour
scheme with black laminate and red
aniline dye legs
38.7 x 87.5 x 60 cm
courtesy of Phillips,
de Pury & Luxembourg

Charles and Ray Eames
OTW (Occasional Table Wood), 1946
manufactured by Molded Plywood
Division of Evans Products Company,
Venice, CA, 1946-1949
molded plywood, walnut veneer
39.4 x 87.5 x 61 cm
courtesy of Phillips,
de Pury & Luxembourg

Herman Miller advertising shot for
moulded plywood furniture by
Charles and Ray Eames
courtesy of Herman Miller

49. Charles and Ray Eames
CTW (Coffee Table Wood), 1946
manufactured by Molded Plywood
Division of Evans Products
Company, Venice, CA, 1946-1947,
Grand Haven, MI, 1947-1948,
Herman Miller, Zeeland MI, 1949-1957
molded plywood, ash veneer
38.1 x 86.4 cm
courtesy of Phillips,
de Pury & Luxembourg

Jean Royère
hall d'un chalet à Megève, 1953-1956
pencil and gouache on Canson paper
courtesy of Musée des Arts décoratifs,
Paris

50. Jean Prouvé
low tables, circa 1950
manufactured by les Ateliers Jean
Prouvé
oak, lacquered steel and stone
80 cm
courtesy of Phillips,
de Pury & Luxembourg

51. Charlotte Perriand and Jean Prouvé
free-form tables, circa 1953
manufactured by les Ateliers
Jean Prouvé
oak and lacquered steel
35.5 x 111.4 cm
courtesy of Phillips,
de Pury & Luxembourg

52. George Nelson Associates
coffee table, model no. 4696, 1949
manufactured by Herman Miller,
Zeeland, MI, 1947-1950
plywood, tubular aluminium,
green linoleum
40.5 x 114 x 64 cm
courtesy of Phillips,
de Pury & Luxembourg

Isamu Kenmochi
coffee table, circa 1955

53. Charles and Ray Eames
ETR (Elliptical Table Rod Base), 1950
manufactured by Herman Miller,
Zeeland, MI, 1951-1964, reissued
1990s-present
plywood, black laminate, steel
25 x 226 cm
Mark Haddawy, Los Angeles
photograph by Richard Goodbody

54. Tapio Wirkkala
coffee table, circa 1958
manufactured by Asko Oy
laminated padouk, maple, hazelwood,
teak and birch
40.5 x 61.5 x 124 cm
courtesy of Wright
Brian Franczyk Photography

55. Tapio Wirkkala
coffee table, model no. 9013,
circa 1958
manufactured by Asko Oy
laminated padouk, maple, hazelwood,
nickel-plated steel and brass
62 x 124.5 x 40 cm
courtesy of Phillips,
de Pury & Luxembourg

56. unknown American designer
coffee table, circa 1950s
possibly manufactured by Lane
plywood, walnut veneer and glass
42 x 150 x 99 cm
collection of Cristina Grajales,
New York
photograph by Richard Goodbody

57. William 'Billy' Haines
Mesa, 1955
ebonised wood and glass
38 x 178 x 135 cm
The Francisco Capelo Collection,
Museu do Design, Lisbon

58. Paul Frankl
coffee table, circa 1950s
manufactured by Johnson Furniture Co,
Grand Rapids, MI
bleached and laminated cork,
mahogany
38 x 104 x 124.5 cm
courtesy of Wright
Brian Franczyk Photography

59. Edward Wormley
coffee table, model no. 5307,
circa 1950s
mahogany, brass-rimmed hole,
rosewood
courtesy of Wright
Brian Franczyk Photography

60. T H Robsjohn-Gibbings
Mesa coffee table, 1950s
manufactured by Widdicomb Furniture
Co, Grand Rapids, MI
laminated birch, sorrel finish
and castors
43.1 x 190 x 137.2 cm
courtesy of Phillips,
de Pury & Luxembourg

61. Vladimir Kagan
coffee table, circa 1950s
manufactured by Kagan-Dreyfuss, Inc,
New York
38 x 152.5 x 86.5 cm
courtesy of Wright
Brian Franczyk Photography

62. Gio Ponti
coffee table, 1953-1954
manufactured by Giordano Chiesa
retailed by Singer & Sons, New York
walnut, brass and tempered glass
39.5 x 100 cm
courtesy of Wright
Brian Franczyk Photography

unknown Italian designer
Coffee Table, circa 1950s
manufactured by Fontana Arte

63. Carlo Mollino
coffee table, circa 1950s
manufactured by Apelli & Varesio,
Turin
retailed by Singer & Sons, New York
maple, brass and glass
147.5 x 132.2 x 59 cm.
courtesy of Phillips,
de Pury & Luxembourg

Carlo Mollino
coffee table with magazine shelf,
from Casa M1, 1944

Carlo Mollino
coffee table from Casa MI, 1944

64. Jacques Adnet
coffee table, circa 1950
in collaboration with Hermés
black leather, brass-plated tubular
steel and glass
46.4 x 95.5 x 41.9 cm
courtesy of Phillips,
de Pury & Luxembourg

Jacques Adnet
Hunting Lodge
published in Décor et Aménagement de
la Maison, 1959

65. Charlotte Perriand
low table, 1941
from the exhibition "Tradition,
Selection, Creation"
Takashimaya department stores,
Tokyo and Osaka, March-May 1941
Unknown wood, dimensions, and
present wherebouts
illustrated in Charlotte Perriand,

"Une Habitation au Japon", *Techniques et Architecture* 6, 1946

66. Charlotte Perriand
table basse
designed 1954, produced in 1984
oak and ebonised wood
courtesy of Musée des Arts décoratifs, Paris

67. George Nakashima
coffee table, model no. 10, 1946
manufactured by Knoll International, 1946-1954
walnut and birch
43 x 85 x 96.5 cm
courtesy of Wright
Brian Franczyk Photography

68. Greta Magnusson Grossman
Coffee Tables, circa 1952
manufactured by Glenn of California, Arcadia, CA
walnut and iron
varying sizes
courtesy of R 20th Century, New York

69. Florence Knoll
Parallel Bars coffee table, model no. 404, 1955
manufactured by Knoll International 1955-1968
walnut and steel
38 x 106.7 cm
courtesy of Knoll Inc.

70. Florence Knoll
coffee table, circa 1950s
manufactured by Knoll International
rosewood and chrome
40.5 x 101.5 x 101.5 cm
courtesy of Wright
Brian Franczyk Photography

71. T H Robsjohn-Gibbings
coffee table, 1950
manufactured by Widdicomb Furniture Co., Grand Rapids, MI
walnut
courtesy of Wright
Brian Franczyk Photography

Allan Gould
coffee table, 1950s
manufactured by Allan Gould Inc, New York
walnut and black-painted iron
illustrated in Roberto Aloi, *Esempi: Tavoli, Tavolini, Carrelli, Seconda Series*, Milan 1955

Poul Kjærholm
PK-61, 1956
manufactured by Kold Christensen 1956-1982, Fritz Hansen 1982-present
rolled marble and chrome-plated steel
32.4 x 82.5 x 82.5 cm
collection of Vance Trimble, New York
photograph by Richard Goodbody

Eero Saarinen
Pedestal 'tulip' coffee tables, 1956
courtesy of Knoll Inc

72. Dan Johnson
prototype coffee table, model B-100, 1958
travertine, black-painted metal and copper
38.1 x 11.8 x 76.2 cm
courtesy of Phillips, de Pury & Luxembourg

73. Arne Jacobsen
coffee table, 1958
manufactured by Fritz Hansen for the Royal Hotel, Copenhagen
wenge and brass
48.2 x 80 cm
courtesy of Phillips, de Pury & Luxembourg

74. Georg Jensen
coffee table, circa 1960
teak
collection of Vance Trimble, New York
photograph Richard Goodbody

75. Sergio Rodrigues
coffee table, circa 1960
manufactured by Oca, São Paulo
rosewood and marble
courtesy of R 20th Century, New York

76. Julio Katinsky
coffee table, 1951-58
manufactured by L'Atelier, São Paulo
plywood, rosewood veneer and iron
117 x 26 cm
courtesy of R 20th Century, New York

77. Edgar Bartolucci and Robert Cato
coffee table, circa 1954
ash, black-painted iron with painted reversible wood panels
38.7 x 151.8 x 47.6 cm
courtesy of Phillips, de Pury & Luxembourg

78. Russel Wright
Trayble, 1950
manufactured by Shwayder Corporation, Denver, CO
retailed by Samsonite
painted metal
collection of James Zemaitis, New York
photograph by Richard Goodbody

Richard Neutra
Camel Table from the Ward House, Beverley Hills, 1961
walnut, bentwood, tubular steel
low position: 36.5 x 177.8 x 99.1 cm
high position: 71.1 x 187.6 x 99.1 cm
courtesy of Phillips, de Pury & Luxembourg

Richard Neutra
Camel Table from the Ward House, North Hollywood, 1940
Photograph courtesy of Julius Shulman

79. Richard Neutra
Camel Table from the Cytron House, Beverly Hills, 1961
walnut, bentwood, tubular steel
low position: 36.5 x 177.8 x 99.1 cm
high position: 71.1 x 187.6 x 99.1 cm
courtesy Phillips, de Pury & Luxembourg

80. Paul László
coffee table, circa 1958
lucite, lacquered wood and castors
51.4 x 201.9 x 80 cm
courtesy of Phillips, de Pury & Luxembourg

Paul László
coffee table in the residence of Mr and Mrs Saks, circa 1958

81. Hendrik van Keppel and Taylor Green
coffee table, circa 1950s
manufactured by Van Keppel-Green, Beverly Hills, CA
painted wood with reversible and interchangeable painted wood panels and glass
40.6 x 134.9 x 91.4 cm
courtesy of Phillips, de Pury & Luxembourg

82. Edward Wormley
coffee table, model no. 5427, circa 1950s
manufactured by Dunbar, Berne, IN
birch, mahogany and glass mosaic
37.2 x 111.8 x 62.2 cm
top extends to 175.3 cm
courtesy of Phillips, de Pury & Luxembourg

photograph from the 1956 Dunbar catalogue

83. Philip and Kelvin Laverne
coffee table, circa 1960s
manufactured by Laverne International, New York
brass, lacquered wood, enameled and acid-etched bronze relief
46.5 x 120 cm
courtesy of Wright
Brian Franczyk Photography

84. Paul Evans
coffee table, circa 1960s
manufactured by Paul Evans Studio, New Hope, PA
retailed by Directional Furniture Co, New York
enameled and welded steel and glass
40.5 x 152.5 x 61 cm
courtesy of Wright
Brian Franczyk Photography

CHAPTER 5

85. Minoru Yamasaki
coffee table, circa 1972
from the Montgomery Ward Headquarters, Chicago
glass, chromed metal
38.1 x 121.9 x 119.7 cm
courtesy of Phillips, de Pury & Luxembourg

Blow up, 1966
courtesy of Philippe Garner

Pierre Paulin
table 877, circa 1960
Pierre Perigault's showroom

86. Roldofo Bonetto
Quattroquarti, model 700, 1969
manufactured by Bernini
ABS plastic
31 x 100 cm
The Francisco Capello Collection, Museo do Design, Lisbon

87. Eero Aarnio
Kantarelli coffee table, circa 1965
manufactured by Asko
ABS plastic

William Plunkett
Selsdon Coffee Table
Nova, September 1966
courtesy of Philippe Garner

88. Angelo Mangiarotti
coffee table, 1959
manufactured by Frigerio, Italy
beola stone

Max Clendinning
living room, 1966-1967

Joe Columbo
central living block of Wohenmodell, 1969
courtesy of Philippe Garner

89. Verner Panton
Ilumesa tables model no. 23600, circa 1970
manufactured by Louis Poulsen

vacuum-molded Cellidor and light
fitting
36 x 72 cm
courtesy of Verner Panton Design

Verner Panton
room design for the Visiona 2, 1970
courtesy of Vernon Panton Design

Pierre Paulin
Pedestal Group, circa 1961-1962

90. Achille and Pier Giacomo
Castiglioni
Rocchetto, 1967
manufactured by Kartell
ABS plastic
38.7 x 59.7cm
courtesy of Phillips,
de Pury & Luxembourg

Verner Panton
Group S420, 1970

91. Warren Platner
Platner coffee table, circa 1960s
manufactured by Knoll International
silvered nickel wire
courtesy of Knoll Inc

92. John Stefanidis
cloud table, circa 1970-1975
manufactured for specific
commissions, London
chromium-plated metal
varying heights
courtesy of John Stefanidis Ltd

93. Cini Boeri
Lunario coffee table, 1972
manufactured by Gavina and Knoll
metal and glass
41.9 x 149.2 x 109.5 cm
courtesy of Phillips,
de Pury & Luxembourg

Vico Magistretti
Caori, in interior, 1962
courtesy of Philippe Garner

94. Gae Aulenti
Jumbo coffee table, 1965
manufactured by Knoll International
1965-1970s
a rare version in nero antico marble
35.9 x 113 x 112.7 cm
courtesy of Phillips,
de Pury & Luxembourg

95. Superstudio
Quaderna, 1972
manufactured by Zanotta
varnished laminate
courtesy of Zanotta

Luigi Colani
Pool Living Pad, 1970-1971
courtesy of Luigi Colani,
www.luigicolani.com

96. Shiro Kuramata
low table, 1976
manufactured by Ishimaru Co Ltd
rubber and glass

97. Shiro Kuramata
Luminous table, 1969
manufactured by Ishimaru Co. Ltd.
opalescent plastic

Allen Jones
low table, 1969
painted fibre glass, leather and glass
courtesy of Philippe Garner

98. George Nakashima
coffee table, 1967
walnut and rosewood butterfly keys
32.7 x 215.9 x 138.8 cm
courtesy of Phillips,
de Pury & Luxembourg

99. George Nakashima
coffee table, 1972
walnut and rosewood butterfly key
33 x 140.3 x 73.5 cm
courtesy of Phillips,
de Pury & Luxembourg

CHAPTER 6

100. Garouste and Bonetti
Ring Table, 1999
prototype
produced By David Gill Editions
polished stainless steel and glass
35 x 140 cm
courtesy of Phillips,
de Pury & Luxembourg

101. Alessandro Mendini
Ondoso, 1980
manufactured by Studio Alchimia
from the Bauhaus 1 collection
iridescent celluloid and colour-
lacquered metal
courtesy of the designer

102. Ettore Sottsass
Park Lane, 1983
manufactured by Memphis
fibre-glass and marble
38 x 109 cm
courtesy of private collection

Miami interior, 2001
Courtesy James Zemaitis

103. Ali Tayar
Nea Table 1, 1995
manufactured by Parallel Design
Partnership
recycled particleboard,
aluminum and glass
33.3 x 121.9 x 101.6 cm
courtesy of the designer and Phillips,
de Pury & Luxembourg

104. Poalo Piva
Alanda, 1982
manufactured by B&B Italia
courtesy of B&B Italia

Wallpaper
Launch issue, September/October 1996

105. Dunne & Raby
Compass Table, 2001
prototype from the Placebo collection
MDF, glass compass needles,
steel and plastic
75 x 75 x 75 cm

106. Gae Aulenti
coffee table, 1980
manufactured by Fontana Arte

107. Rei Kawakubo
a pair of Grey Triangle Tables,
circa 1985
manufactured by Pallucco for
Comme des Garçons
polished and semi-polished granite
and iron bases castors
43.2 x 119.4 x 89.2 cm (together)
courtesy of Phillips,
de Pury & Luxembourg

108. Shin + Tomoko Azumi
Table = Chest, 1999
produced by Shin + Tomoko Azumi
beech veneered plywood
40 x 40 x 90 cm
courtesy of Shin + Tomoko Azumi,
mail@azumi.co.uk
photograph © Thomas Dobbie

109. Hector Serrano & Lola Llorca
From Infinity to Beyond, 2001
steel, rubber, foam and fabric
30 x 120 x 100 cm
courtesy of Lola Llorca & Hector
Serrano, www.hectorserrano.com

110. Jerszy Seymour
freewheelin' franklin, 2000
remote controlled table
limited edition series
manufactured by Sputnik/Idée
courtesy of Jerszy Seymour

111. Barber Osgerby
Loop Table, 1997
manufactured by Isokon
Plus/Cappellini
laminated birch plywood
23 x 135 x 60 cm
courtesy of Barber Osgerby

112. El Ultimo Grito
Mind the Gap, 1998
manufactured by Punt Mobiles
steel and synthetic rubber
35 x 80 x 60 cm
courtesy El Ultimo Grito

113. Danny Lane
Tagliatelle, 1997
25 mm glass and stainless steel
42.5 x 237 x 145 cm
main photograph
photographer Peter Hood
side view photograph
photographer Stephen Spellar
courtesy of Danny Lane

114. Marcel Wanders
Smoke, 2000
smoked glass and clear glass
manufactured by Capellini
40 x 100 x 100 cm (large version)
40 x 100 x 60 cm (small version)
courtesy of Marcel Wanders

115. Michael Young
Wagon, 2000
manufactured by Magis
injection-moulded zylar, polyurethane
and die cast aluminium
12 x 68 x 30 cm
courtesy of Michael Young

116. Lorenzo Damiani
Tavolante table and light, 1999
prototype
polytelen and steel
30 x 120 x 200 cm
courtesy of Lorenzo Damiani

117. Ron Arad
B.O.O.P. (Blown Out Of Proportion),
1998
unique pieces
produced The Gallery Mourmans
polished stainless steel
courtesy of Ron Arad associates

118. Shin + Tomoko Azumi
hm30 low table, 2001
manufactured by Hitch Mylius
courtesy of Shin + Tomoko Azumi

119. Michael Young
MY07 Magazine Table, 1995
manufactured by EBY Co Japan /
MY 022 UK
pu and aluminium
47 x 48 x 35 cm
courtesy of Michael Young

120. Michael Sodeau
Flip, 1999/2000
manufactured by Isokon Plus
birch
courtesy of Michael Sodeau

121. Karim Rashid
Nauge Coffee Table, 2000
Manufactured by Elite
glass, stainless steel
courtesy of Karim Rashid

122. The Campana Brothers
Inflatable Table, 2001
manufactured by Museum of Modern Art,
NY
polyvinylchloride film and anodised
aluminium
45 x 40 cm
courtesy of The Campana Brothers
photograph by Andrés Otero

123. Marcel Wanders
Lace Table, 1997
manufactured by Droog Design
epoxy glass and Swiss lace
courtesy of Marcel Wanders

124. The Campana Brothers
Cardboard table, 2001
manufactured by The Campana
Brothers/ Edra
corrugated cardboard and metal
44 x 136 x 50 cm
courtesy of Edra

125. Antonio Citterio
Solo, 2002
manufactured by B&B Italia
courtesy of B&B Italia

126. Michael Sodeau
Satellite Table, 1997
produced by MSP
macassar ebony or rosewood veneer and
turned aluminium or red, white or blue
finish
32 x 36 x 36 cm
courtesy of Michael Sodeau

127. Marcel Wanders
Knotted Table, 2001
manufactured by Cappellini
parabeam, fibreglass-reinforced
fabric, carbon, aramide, epoxy resin
and mirror
52 x 90 cm
courtesy of Marcel Wanders

128. Michael Young
Yogi, 2002
manufactured by Magis
rotation-moulded polyurethane
25 x 60 cm diameter
courtesy of Michael Young

129. Nick Crosbie/Inflate
Magnet Coffee Table, 2001
prototype
courtesy of Inflate

130. Ron Arad
coffee table, 1991
produced by One-Off Ltd
unique
polished stainless steel
170 x 280 x 24 cm
courtesy of Phillips,
de Pury & Luxembourg

131.
Joan Gasper
Sydney, 2000
prototype
aluminium
30 x 150 x 75 cm
courtesy of Joan Gasper

132. The Campana Brothers
Tatoo, 2001
manufactured by Fontana Arte, Milan,
Italy
stainless steel and PVC
71 x 150 x 150 cm
courtesy of The Campana Brothers
photograph by Andrés Otero

133. Martin Szekely
M.G.D., 2002
produced by Galerie Kreo
limited edition of six pieces and
two artist's proofs
polished steel and lacquered
aluminium
36 x 60 x 130 cm
© Marc Domage
courtesy of Galerie Kreo

Acknowledgments

We would both like to thank Duncan McCorquodale and all at Black Dog for their time, patience and this opportunity, Paul Khera and Maria Beddoes for the design, all our colleagues at Phillips, de Pury and Luxembourg in London and New York, Richard Goodbody and Wit McKay for their superb photography, and a very special thanks to our colleagues Philippe Garner, Victoria Rodriguez Thiessen and Megan Whippen for their constant help, ideas and support.

Alexander would like to thank the following people for their help, advice and support: Shin and Tomoko Azumi, Daniel Brooke, Francisco Capelo, Mark Harding, Byron Slater, my parents, sister and the rest of my family, my friends and beautiful Bun.

James would like to thank the following for their advice, leads, love and good vibes: Jennifer Avallon, W John Bauer, Caroline Baumann, Joanne Creveling, Evan and Zesty, Dennis Freedman, Cara Greenberg, Mark Haddawy, Philip Keller, Cary Leitzes, Susan Magrino, Liz O'Brien, Mitchell Owens, Janis Staggs-Flinchum, Charles Venable, John Waddell, Richard Wright and my late parents.

Black Dog Publishing. London. New York. ©2003 Black Dog Publishing Limited, the artists and authors. All rights reserved

Written by Alexander Payne and James Zemaitis. Picture research by William Turner and Julian Ball. Additional research by Jennifer Birnbaum. Production by Duncan McCorquodale and Catherine Grant. Designed at PKMB

Black Dog Publishing Limited, 5 Ravenscroft Street, London E2 7SH, UK. Tel: +44 (0)20 7613 1922. Fax: +44 (0)20 7613 1944. Email: info@bdp.demon.co.uk

PO Box 20035, Greenley Square Station, New York NY 10001-0001, USA. Tel: +212 684 2140. Fax: +212 684 3583. www.bdpworld.com

All opinions expressed within this publication are those of the authors and not necessarily of the publisher.

British Library Cataloguing-in-Publication Data. A catalogue record for this book is available from the British Library. ISBN 1 901033 04 X